Clare of Assisi
THE LETTERS TO AGNES

Joan Mueller, O.S.F.

A Michael Glazier Book

LITURGICAL PRESS
Collegeville, Minnesota

www.litpress.org

A Michael Glazier Book published by the Liturgical Press

Cover design by Ann Blattner. Icon by Simone Martini.

The translation from Latin of St. Clare's letters as published in this book is the work of Sr. Joan Mueller, O.S.F.

1   2   3   4   5   6   7   8

Library of Congress Cataloging-in-Publication Data

Mueller, Joan, 1956–
    Clare of Assisi : the letters to Agnes / Joan Mueller.
      p. cm.
    ISBN 0-8146-5168-2 (alk. paper)
    1. Clare, of Assisi, Saint, 1194–1253—Correspondence.
    2. Agnes, Princess of Bohemia, 1205–1282—Correspondence.
    3. Christian saints—Italy—Assisi—Correspondence.
    4. Franciscan nuns—Spiritual life. I. Title: Letters to Agnes.
    II. Clare, of Assisi, Saint, 1194–1253. Correspondence.
    English. Selections. III. Title.

BX4700.C6M84 2003
271'.97302—dc21

                                            2002043349

In gratitude for their courage and inspiration,
this book is dedicated to and its royalties will be given to

THE WOMEN OF THE UPPER ROOM
CATHOLIC WORKER HOUSE

in Passaic Park, New Jersey

Contents

Preface

This book was born out of conversations. Fr. André Cirino, O.F.M., who was one of the founding leaders of the Franciscan pilgrimage to Prague, expressed the desperate need for well-researched resources in English on the letters of St. Clare to Agnes and on Agnes of Prague herself. At the time, I was writing a book for St. Bonaventure University Press on Clare's letters, but had not finished it. André and I happened to meet in Assisi before he was scheduled to go to Prague, and we spent long hours talking and preparing notes for his pilgrimage. I realized during these conversations that the academic book I was preparing might not have been helpful to pilgrims who were searching for a spiritual rather than an academic experience of the early Franciscan sisters. A more accessible text would be needed.

A few years later, I had finished the book for St. Bonaventure's and was speaking with Secular Franciscan, Jim Himes, of Franciscan Resources. Jim also asked for a book on Clare's letters that would be a more user-friendly approach to the topic. Another style was necessary for formation groups, women's spirituality groups, and reading groups.

My own college and graduate students also needed a more approachable way to learn to love Clare. They wanted the opportunity to reflect on key questions that would help make her story and spirituality come to life.

As a result, I had the honor to write this book. Since Clare wrote four letters to Agnes, the reader will find that each of the four letters is formatted as a chapter. Each chapter contains an introduction to the letter being presented, the text of the letter itself, an essay exploring the context of Clare's letters, and some thoughts on the contemporary relevance of the letter. This is followed by reflection/sharing questions for personal integration and group discussion.

I have left all footnotes and endnotes out of this text. Those who are interested in the manuscript tradition of Clare's letters and the sources behind the information presented here are invited to consult my text *Clare's Letters to Agnes: Texts and Sources* (St. Bonaventure, N.Y.: The Franciscan Institute, 2001). There they will find a plethora of notes and information to satisfy their academic questions.

My research on Clare's letters was funded through grants given by the Franciscan Sisters of Joy, the Graduate School and the College of Arts and Sciences of Creighton University, and the Chicago Poor Clare Endowment Fund. I am grateful to Paige McDonald who translated hundreds of background documents necessary to this project. I am also indebted to Dr. Mary Kuhlman, Fran Minear, and Sr. Christine Stevenson, O.S.F., who graciously proofread this text.

After five years of academic research on these letters, it was a privilege for me to sit back and write a book whose focus was finding the heart of Clare as she wrote to her dear friend, Agnes. Of course, since Clare is inviting Agnes into the depths of trinitarian union in her letters, no reader can ever be their ultimate master. All one can hope for is the academic discipline not to misinterpret Clare's words, and the spiritual courage to follow Clare's instructions, as Agnes did, in joyfully giving God everything. This can be done, as Clare insists, because we know that God is more lavish in giving than we can ever hope to be.

I am confident that prayer groups, formation groups, discussion groups, and spirituality classes will discover depths of Clare's letters that I have not, and this is a cause for great joy! My hope is that these good people will remember this author in their prayers.

The Feast of St. Clare

August 11, 2003

Introduction

Moderns are fascinated with the writings of medieval religious women. This is true not only for those interested in these writings for their religious teachings, but also for secular readers interested in the history of women. Medieval religious women offer a glimpse on medieval Church, society, and family that presents a needed balance to the male, monastic or scholastic experience. Religious women of the Middle Ages were as religiously committed, and in many cases even more religiously dedicated than their male counterparts, and yet, did not share the same institutional benefits. Perhaps because of this, their religious zeal and tenacious commitment is strangely appealing to moderns. We want to know their secret. We want to know the fire that burned in their hearts.

Because they were not as enmeshed in the political and temporal struggles of their age, the voices of medieval women offer a kind of timeless solace. Many contemporaries bask in the insight of Julian of Norwich's concept of the motherhood of Christ, and for the most part ignore the great Bernard of Clairvaux who offered a similar insight in a male key. Others laugh at the practical humor of Teresa of Avila as she journeys through the mansions of her *Interior Castle*. Still others nod as though they were acquainted with the writings of Catherine of Siena, even though most have only read a few of her letters or some of her prayers. Many modern readers feel that they have a sense of these great women, almost as if they know them intuitively.

In the midst of the modern revival of women's medieval writings, the letters of Clare of Assisi have for the most part been left undiscovered. This is true for many reasons. There is the familiar joke that there are three things that God does not know. These three things are: (1) What is a Dominican *really* thinking?; (2) What is a Jesuit *really* doing?; and finally, (3) *How many* orders of Franciscans are there? Certainly in many places in the world, there seems to be a different Franciscan women's community on every corner. Because there are so many, the struggle for Franciscan women to promote, organize, accept, and include the opinions of women outside of their own small communities has been difficult. In addition, Clare's enthusiasm for following Christ in corporate as well as personal poverty is not shared by all.

The order that Clare founded is still very much alive and well today. Because many Poor Clares still remain cloistered, even strictly cloistered, there is a sense among some scholars that they might misunderstand the contemplative experience and that there will be real, living people who will know that they have it wrong. It is not the role of the Poor Clares to produce women with doctorates in history or theology. While other Franciscan women might have the Ph.D. in these fields, there is the hesitancy to write if one does not know whether one is able to blend correctly the intellectual and the charismatic.

If these issues are overcome, there is the problem of Clare herself. While Julian of Norwich and even Teresa of

Avila are moderately easy for moderns to pick up and read, Catherine of Siena and certainly Clare of Assisi must be read in social and historical context. Only then can their words be "translated" into modern sensibilities.

This insight was brought home to me one day while I was giving a retreat to a group of Franciscan sisters. Knowing of my love for St. Clare, one of the sisters approached me hesitantly and, almost with the sense of unburdening her conscience, whispered to me saying, "I really don't like St. Clare." "Why?," I asked her. "Because she was so stuck on poverty," was the reply. I wanted to congratulate this sister for having the courage to express what so many others cannot. Without understanding the context of Clare's words, it is difficult for moderns to appreciate Clare's love affair with poverty. Most adults understand deep in their souls the simple axiom that poverty is romantic only to those who haven't experienced it!

Given the current popularity of medieval religious women, contemporaries at times forget that these women truly did belong to another era and to other cultures. Because of this, the writings of medieval women need to be not only translated but also contextualized. In the case of Clare's letters, there are two medieval women whose culture and social backgrounds must be examined.

Clare of Assisi

St. Clare was born in 1193 or 1194 in the town of Assisi. She was the daughter of Offreduccio di Favarone and his wife, Ortolana. Caught in the thirteenth-century crossfire between the long-established noble families and the "new money" merchant class, Clare and her noble family fled the riots of Assisi to the neighboring city of Perugia where noble supremacy was still honored. When Assisi negotiated terms of peace between the nobles and merchants, Clare and her family returned to their palace in Assisi next to the Cathedral of San Rufino.

On the other side of the conflict was the young merchant, Francis, son of Pietro Bernardone of Assisi. Longing to become a great knight, Francis battled against Perugia, was captured, and was subsequently imprisoned for one year in Perugia. He returned home to Assisi sick, disoriented, and despondent. The life of carousing and partying with his friends that he had been locally famous for before his imprisonment no longer gave him joy. Unable to endure the confines of his father's luxury cloth store, Francis, trying to find solace for his disillusioned soul in prayer and in the beauty of nature, escaped to high wooded mountains and secluded caves. Eventually he decided to renounce his inheritance and to embrace a life of peace, prayer, and simple work.

Other men in Assisi, tired of violence, followed him. Eventually they wrote a simple agreement concerning their choice of lifestyle made up of Gospel verses. Desiring permission to preach to others about the peace they had found, the small group went to Rome to present themselves and their project to Pope Innocent III. Seeing Francis's talent as a preacher, and needing orthodox preachers who could combat heresy by entertaining the masses with popular preaching in town squares and churches, Innocent III gave them oral approval to preach.

After Francis and his brothers returned from Rome, Clare heard Francis preach. Clare and Francis had both grown up with and experienced firsthand the consequences of violence, riots, ambushes, and battles. Their families had grown rich off the backs of the poor. The youth of Assisi was losing heart with the constant struggle to have more and more. While the appetite of their fathers was insatiable, the sons and daughters of Assisi seemed to be sickened by the very thought of continuing the gluttonous struggle to acquire more.

Clare was a noble woman and so understood the struggle a bit differently than Francis. Clare had learned the art of being a noble wife from her mother Ortolana. She was destined to marry a man who would advance the wealth and power of her family. This man would use the work of the poor to his advantage, plot the destruction of others, ride out to battle and kill, perhaps rape or permit the rape of the women of his adversary, and then come home again to Clare. As Clare imagined her future, the road to preserving the old wealth and honor of her family would be a costly one.

This social context makes Francis's and Clare's choice of poverty understandable. In an era when families fought families, and churchmen and monastics were entering into litigation to protect and expand wealth, Assisi's children saw that they had no future if they continued the behavior of their parents. If Francis had taken the way of his father, he probably would have died on a battlefield without singing for the world his *Canticle of Creation.* If Clare had not run away from the prison of her noble palazzo, she might have ended her days as a widow grieving over her husband and sons who died on some field for a senseless purpose. Instead, Francis, the merchant, and Clare, the noblewoman, made another choice.

They called their choice "poverty." Poverty, rather than wealth, would be their salvation. They were not original in proposing this ideal. Many laypeople, religious, and clerics saw the corruption of church and society and knew that both institutions needed to curb their gluttonous behavior. The greed of parents was killing their children. The greed of cities was inviting destruction. The greed of the Church was undermining its spiritual credibility and exposing it to scandal.

Clare escaped from her home to the tiny church of Saint Mary of the Angels where Francis and his fledgling group of brothers were staying. No doubt because of the persistence of Clare, Bishop Guido of Assisi knew and perhaps even facilitated her escape. After Francis had tonsured Clare, making her unmarriageable, he and his brothers took her by night to the Benedictine monastery of San Paolo delle Abbadesse. This powerful monastery had obtained the privilege of threatening excommunication against anyone who harmed its inhabitants. Knowing that the knights in Clare's family would be furious when they discovered her disappearance, the bishop of Assisi and Francis knew that Clare needed to be in a place where she would be safe.

The knights did come to the monastery and demanded to have Clare returned to them. Clinging to the altar cloth of the monastic church, Clare bared her tonsured head. Seeing that she would no longer be of value as a bride, the knights of Clare's family left with confused rage, disowning her. Without a family to claim her, Clare was now free to leave the Benedictine monastery to begin her Franciscan life.

Just outside the confines of Assisi, the brothers were probably still working on rebuilding the small Monastery of San Damiano that Clare would call "home" for the rest of her life. Clare moved temporarily to the Monastery of Sant' Angelo di Panzo, a small community of beguine-like women—women who lived a quasi-religious lifestyle often without an official rule—near San Damiano. While she was there, Clare's sister, Catherine, also escaped the family home and found her way to Sant'Angelo. The knights of the Offreduccio family came after Catherine, and when she did not cooperate, they beat her until she seemed lifeless. Clare nursed her back to health, and Clare and Catherine, who was given the religious name of Agnes by Francis, entered the Monastery of San Damiano.

Agnes of Prague

Born in 1211, Agnes of Prague was the youngest daughter of King Přemysl Otakar I and Queen Constance of Hungary. Her father was a master politician who secured for Bohemia a medieval dynasty. Always anxious to enrich and enlarge his kingdom, Otakar betrothed his daughters diplomatically.

At the age of eight, Agnes was betrothed to Henry VII, the son of the German emperor Frederick II. Henry was being educated in Austria at the time, so Agnes was sent to Vienna to begin her formation as queen. Agnes's future seemed secure until her host, Leopold VI of Austria undermined Otakar's agreement with Frederick and negotiated a marriage between his own daughter, Margaret, and Henry. Agnes was sent back to Bohemia, and Otakar declared war on Leopold VI in retaliation for his audacious attempt to undercut Bohemia's regional supremacy.

With Bohemia's alliance with Germany compromised, Otakar I refocused his efforts on securing an alliance with England. Henry III, king of England, was proposed as a possible suitor for Agnes. Otakar dragged his feet, most likely holding out for a more lucrative offer.

It came from Emperor Frederick II himself, Henry VII's father. Recently widowed and wanting to thwart the plans of the English, Frederick II asked for Agnes's hand. Agnes, however, was formulating other plans for her life. Knowing

that Pope Gregory IX was doing all within his power to keep
Frederick's power at bay, she appealed to the Pope for help.
After the death of her father, Agnes's brother, Wenceslas I—
not "Good King Wenceslas" but one of his descendants—
could now decide the issue. Agnes pleaded with him, and
Wenceslas informed Frederick of Agnes's refusal.

Agnes's cousin, Elizabeth of Hungary, who was only
slightly older than Agnes, died on November 17, 1231, at
the age of twenty-four. Elizabeth had founded a hospital for
the sick and the poor, and her care of famine victims was well
known. In a mere four and one-half years, Gregory IX would
canonize her.

No doubt inspired by Elizabeth's example, Agnes was
now free of political marriage proposals and was able to follow a dream of her own. In 1233, Agnes built a hospital with
her royal dowry and placed it in the hands of a pious lay
brotherhood, the Crosiers of the Red Star. Next, Agnes built
a monastery for women and a small convent for the friars who
would be their providers and chaplains. Inspired by the stories
of the friars in Prague and by the Franciscan example of St.
Elizabeth, Agnes sent messengers to Rome asking for papal
protection for her monastery. She also requested sisters who
followed the form of life of Clare's sisters at San Damiano.
Clare sent Agnes five German-speaking sisters from Trent.

On June 11, 1234, the twenty-three-year-old Agnes entered the monastery that she herself had founded. At the cere-
mony were seven bishops and her brother, King Wenceslas I.

Why Choose Poverty?

If one believes that grace builds on nature, then it must
be admitted and even celebrated that every vocation has both

spiritual and temporal advantages. This practical and even prosaic dimension of vocational calling has been reflected upon little in modern times.

The need to stress the practical dimension of a religious vocation is perhaps more understandable if one reflects upon this truth within the context of marriage. If a marriage is contemplated between a man and a woman, their families and even their church communities will ask very practical questions. "What does the other do for a living?" "What is the other's family like?" "Is the other a basically moral person?" "What is the other's intent regarding financial exigency, children, place of residence, etc.?" In other words, marriage, even in our very liberal culture, is not based on hormones alone. In the best of circumstances it is grounded in attraction but also on practical considerations. People feel good about going to a wedding when the love between two people is based on a firm, practical foundation.

The same is true in religious life. Yes, there needs to be a strong spiritual attraction. Candidates must have the generosity and desire to give themselves totally to God. Yet, because we are human beings and not angels, this generosity must be grounded in very practical considerations. In other words, one must live one's religious vocation day after day in the concreteness of everyday life.

The ability to sustain these daily practicalities is as important to the discernment of a religious vocation as is the spiritual attraction. Sisters will ask a candidate practical questions. "Are you attracted to living a poor lifestyle?" "Is chastity a burden or a gift for you?" "Do you enjoy living with our sisters in community?" Sisters celebrate a candidate's profession more fully when the spiritual desires of the one being professed have been demonstrated within the context of daily life.

Why did the thirteenth century produce so many vocations, and why were women attracted to the poverty of the Franciscan Order? It seems that the answer might be found in contemplating the practical situation. If she had not joined Francis, Clare would probably have been married to a nobleman of her family's choosing with all the violence and tragedy that accompanied such a lifestyle. Agnes would have been married to Emperor Frederick II, a man well known for his womanizing who was often at odds with, and even during some periods in his life excommunicated by, the pope. Both Clare and Agnes found in their choice of religious life a kind of peace that they would not have had in the marriages that were being planned for them.

Yet, Clare and Agnes's choice went beyond the ordinary decision for religious life. Both Assisi and Prague were well populated with wealthy and stable monastic establishments for women. Why not join a monastery like San Paolo delle Abbadesse near Assisi or like Saint George's royal monastery in Prague and enjoy the peace, wealth, and security that they provided?

The answer to this question helps us to understand Clare and Agnes's attraction to poverty. The established monasteries at the time were part of the feudal economy that was being challenged by the new merchant class and that often lived off the backs of the poor. Monastic endowments were usually given in the form of land grants. The rights to these properties included, besides the land, control over the serfs living off the land, water rights, road tolls, lumber, crops, and animals. Without state control to negotiate communal welfare, those who owned property essentially dictated the kind of life that the poor would have.

It was not uncommon for a diocesan bishop to fight with canons, monks, and nuns over property rights. Property was power in the medieval world. Those who owned property dictated the conditions under which the poor would live and die.

The Franciscan insight was not merely to provide for the poor out of the monastic coffers, but rather to join the ranks of the poor. Francis's first follower, Bernard, did this by going to the Hospital of San Giorgio and giving his entire fortune to the poor and the sick who were living there. Elizabeth and Agnes, who had the considerable wealth of royal dowries, gave everything they had to the poor by building hospitals for the sick, indigent, and homeless. This act, if it happened on a large scale, had the potential to turn the economy of Europe upside down. In joining the Franciscan lifestyle, resources that once belonged to the rich now belonged to the poor. The rich became poor, and the poor were able to survive. Through their choice of poverty, Agnes and Clare's lives would make a difference in the lives of others.

Questions for Reflection/Sharing

1. Which writings of medieval women have you previously read? Why are you attracted to these women? What have you learned from them?
2. Do the stories of the lives of Clare and Agnes relate in any way to the story of your own life?
3. Do you agree that vocational choices should be guided by practicalities as well as by the attractions of our hearts? How did the dance between attraction and practicality play itself out in your own vocational choice?

Clare's First Letter to Agnes

INTRODUCTION

Most likely Clare of Assisi wrote her first letter to Agnes of Prague in the summer of 1234. On June 11, 1234, Pentecost Sunday of that year, Agnes of Prague, with numerous bishops and dignitaries in attendance, entered the Franciscan monastery in Prague that she herself had built. Associated with this monastery was a hospital that Agnes had also established in order to take care of the needs of Prague's poor. Since, after the example of Francis's first companion, Bernard, the first step for entering the Franciscan Order was to sell everything that one had and give it to the poor, Agnes gave away her royal dowry by founding this hospital and monastery.

Agnes had heard about Clare from the Franciscan brothers who had come to Prague. These brothers had been well received by Prague's noble families. Inspired by the stories that they told concerning the example of Clare of Assisi and by the example of her cousin St. Elizabeth, Agnes decided to embrace the Franciscan way of life.

Since her childhood, Agnes's father, King Otakar I, had engaged her to a number of European suitors with the intent of advancing his kingdom. When Emperor Frederick II himself set his eyes on a political marriage with the kingdom of Bohemia and asked for Agnes's hand in the spring of 1228, Agnes appealed to Pope Gregory IX. Frederick, however, was undaunted, and in 1233 seems to have asked again for Agnes's hand. It was only after the death of her father that Agnes was able to persuade her brother, King Wenceslaus I, to allow her to begin her life as a Franciscan.

The news of Agnes's decision to reject Frederick II's proposal reverberated throughout Europe. Clare wrote her first letter to congratulate Agnes on her choice and to invite her into the poverty that she saw as the essence of the Franciscan lifestyle. Her first letter is a hymn celebrating Agnes's "sacred exchange," the giving up of the things of time for the things of eternity." Because Christ chose poverty in taking on human flesh, Agnes is wise in giving up her riches in order to embrace the Poor Christ who has promised the kingdom of heaven to the poor.

CLARE'S FIRST LETTER

(1) To Lady Agnes, venerable and most holy virgin, daughter of the most renowned and illustrious king of Bohemia, (2) Clare, her subject and handmaid in all circumstances, an unworthy servant of Jesus Christ and the useless handmaid of the enclosed ladies of the Monastery of San Damiano, commends herself in every way and sends, with special respect, the wish that Agnes attain the glory of everlasting happiness.

(3) Hearing the news, which brings you the highest honor, of your holy conversion and manner of life—news that has been reputably disseminated not only to me but to nearly every region of the world—I rejoice and exalt exceedingly in the Lord. (4) Concerning this news, I am not the only one who rejoices, but I am joined by all those who serve and desire to serve Jesus Christ.

(5) I rejoice because you, more than others—having had the opportunity to become legitimately married with eminent glory to the illustrious emperor as would befit your and his pre-eminence—could have enjoyed public ostentation, honors, and worldly status. (6) Spurning all these things with your whole heart and mind, you have chosen instead holiest poverty and physical want, (7) accepting a nobler spouse, the Lord Jesus Christ, who will keep your virginity always immaculate and inviolate.

(8) Having loved him, you are chaste;
having touched him, you will be made more pure;
having received him, you are a virgin.

(9) His power is stronger,
his nobility higher,
his appearance lovelier,
his love sweeter,
and his every grace more elegant.

(10) You are now held tightly in the embrace
of the one
who has adorned your breast with precious stones
and has hung priceless pearls from your ears.

(11) He has completely covered you with
glittering and sparkling gems,
and has placed on your head a golden crown
engraved with the seal of holiness.

(12) Therefore, dearest sister—or should I say, most venerable lady, because you are spouse and mother and sister of my Lord Jesus Christ, (13) and are most resplendently distinguished by the banner of inviolable virginity and holiest poverty—be strengthened in the holy service begun in you out of a burning desire for the Poor Crucified. (14) For all of us he endured the passion of the cross, rescuing us from the power of the prince of darkness—by whose power we were kept in chains because of the transgression of our first parent—and reconciling us to God the Father.

    (15) O blessed poverty
        that provides eternal riches to those who
        love and embrace it!
    (16) O holy poverty,
        God promises the kingdom of heaven
        and, of course,
        gives eternal glory and a happy life
        to those who possess and desire it!
    (17) O noble poverty
        that the Lord Jesus Christ, who ruled
        and is ruling heaven and earth,
        and who spoke and all things were made,
        chose to embrace before anything else!

(18) For foxes have dens, scripture says, and the birds of the sky have nests, but the Son of Man, who is Christ, has nowhere to lay his head; instead, bowing his head, he handed over his spirit.

(19) If, then, such a great Lord when coming into the virgin's womb chose to appear contemptible, needy, and poor in this world (20) so that human beings, who were utterly poor and needy, suffering from a dire lack

4

of heavenly food, might be made rich in him by means of the kingdom of heaven that they will indeed possess, (21) exalt exceedingly and rejoice, filled with great joy and spiritual happiness. (22) Because—since contempt of the world has pleased you more than its honors; poverty more than temporal riches; and storing up treasures in heaven rather than on earth (23) where neither rust consumes them, nor moth destroys them, and thieves do not dig them up and steal them—your most abundant reward is in heaven, (24) and you have quite fittingly deserved to be called sister, spouse, and mother of the Son of the Most High Father and the glorious Virgin.

(25) For, I am sure that you know that the kingdom of heaven is promised and given by the Lord only to the poor, because as long as something temporal is the object of love, the fruit of charity is lost. (26) You know, too, that a person cannot serve God and material wealth, since either the one is loved and the other hated, or the person will serve one and despise the other. (27) You also know that a person wearing clothing cannot fight with another who is naked, because the one who has something that might be grasped is more quickly thrown to the ground.

(28) You know also that it is not possible for a person to remain glorious in the world and to reign with Christ in heaven; and that a camel will be able to pass through the eye of a needle before a rich person ascends into the kingdom of heaven. (29) These are the reasons why you disposed of your clothing, I mean your worldly wealth, so that you might have the strength not to succumb completely to the one struggling against you, and might enter the kingdom of heaven by the narrow road and constricted gate.

(30) It is indeed a great and praiseworthy exchange
   to give up the temporal for the eternal,
   to merit the heavenly rather than the earthly,
   to receive a hundredfold instead of one,
   to have a happy, everlasting life.

(31) Given that you want to be strengthened in his holy service growing from good to better, from virtue to virtue, I thought, therefore, that I should do all I can to implore Your Excellency and Holiness with humble prayers in the innermost heart of Christ, (32) so that the one to whose service you devote yourself with every desire of your mind may choose to bestow freely upon you the rewards you have desired.

(33) I also beseech you in the Lord, as best as I can, to be so kind as to include in your most holy prayers me, your servant, although useless, and the other sisters who are devoted to you who live with me in the monastery. (34) By the help of your prayers, may we be able to merit the mercy of Jesus Christ so that we, together with you, may deserve to enjoy the ever-lasting vision.

(35) Farewell in the Lord, and please pray for me.

CONTEXT

It's a long way from Assisi to Prague, but the Franciscan brothers knew the journey well. In the early summer of 1234, a Franciscan friar assigned to Trent, or to another destination north, had climbed from the friary of Saint Mary of the Angels in the valley of Assisi up the lower portion of Mount Subasio to the Monastery of San Damiano.

We know from the closing of Clare's fourth letter that Clare and her sisters knew the Franciscan brothers who carried letters for them. While climbing the slope up to the Monastery of San Damiano, the brother messenger was most probably looking forward to receiving words of encouragement from the famous Sister Clare. Clare, known for her holiness even before her decision to follow St. Francis, was renowned as a saintly woman and as a healer. The small slope toward San Damiano was quickly traversed, and the brother found himself in the monastery parlor.

We do not know who carried Clare's first letter to Agnes into northern Italy, over the Alps, and on to Prague. It probably arrived in Prague in the summer or early fall of 1234. There Agnes and her small community of noble women received it with great joy from a Franciscan brother. They most likely took it into the monastery refectory and read it aloud with great devotion.

The Salutation

Verses 1–2 of Clare's letter are, of course, the salutation. In English we would simply say, "to my dear friend, Agnes, from Clare." One can compare ancient and medieval salutations to an email address. They begin with "to" and end with "from."

The tenor of the medieval salutation was to show respectful deference to the recipient. Clare calls herself an "unworthy servant of Jesus Christ" and a "useless handmaid," but we should not over spiritualize Clare's show of humility here. A little self-depreciation in the salutation was simply the style in which a medieval letter was written.

In the salutation, Clare describes her community as "the enclosed ladies of the Monastery of San Damiano." Many medieval women lived in enclosed and semi-enclosed situations. In order to preserve the virginity and therefore the marriageability of the women in their families, noble lords built sumptuous palaces where their daughters lived and for the most part remained out of the public eye. When they were of age, these daughters would be bartered to lords whose family assets and alliance would increase the wealth and power of the family.

Clare grew up in this way, learning from her mother, Ortolana, how to embroider, read, and take care of a household. In thirteenth-century Italy, when the pope was fighting against the emperor, one city against a neighboring city, and one warlord against another, every prudent means was used to protect women from being caught in the crossfire. Since even nuns were often the targets of pillage and rape, the holiness, silence, and enclosure of monastic women were seen as a protection. If a monastery was pillaged, nuns known for the silence and integrity of their enclosure might at least hope for the sympathy of the people.

There were also, however, thirteenth-century women who had issues with imposed enclosure. Some women engaged in preaching, which before contemporary media was as much about entertainment and politics as it was about religion. Political views that went counter to ecclesiastical politics were aired in town squares by men and women. In some Christian sects that opposed the rule of Rome, women were ordained and functioned not only as preachers but also as sacramental ministers.

The law of enclosure required monastic women to embrace a specific kind of religious economy. Women who entered enclosed monasteries were usually required to bring a dowry sufficient enough to provide for their lifelong needs. If this dowry was given in the form of land, which it often was, it would be used as an endowment that provided annual revenues from crops, orchards, roads, water rights and other goods. Although it does not seem that Clare in any way objected to enclosure because it would prohibit her from sacramental functions, we will see that she vehemently objected to what was seen as the standard economics of enclosure.

In all of Clare's letters the point of the letter, or one could even say the summary of her letter, is found at the very end of her salutations. In the first letter, Clare's objective is a simple one. Clare writes with the hope "that Agnes attain the glory of everlasting happiness." We will see that Clare believes that this happiness is not something that Agnes will attain only after she crosses over into the heavenly realm. Rather, because of Agnes's choice to enter the monastery, her happiness will begin immediately. Throughout her letters, Clare will teach Agnes how to embrace this path of joy.

The Gossip Concerning Agnes's Entrance

Clare next talks about the public "buzz" concerning Agnes's decision to enter the Franciscan lifestyle. Agnes is a princess who was engaged to be married to the Holy Roman Emperor himself. She could have literally had it all. Instead, she joins a monastery—but not just any monastery. Agnes decides to join the fledgling Franciscan Order whose founder had recently died and whose brothers were struggling, awkwardly at times, to establish their identity. Moreover, the women associated with the Franciscan Order were in a kind of complicated legal limbo.

In 1215, the Fourth Lateran Council decreed that no new religious rules were to be written. Canon thirteen of this council says: "Lest too great a variety of religious orders leads to grave confusion in God's church, we strictly forbid anyone henceforth to found a new religious order. Whoever wants to become a religious should enter one of the already approved orders." Clare had just entered San Damiano with her sister Agnes a few years before 1215. Francis seems not to have been affected by the legislation because he had obtained oral approval for the form of life of the brothers in 1209.

From the beginning, Clare saw herself as a Franciscan. The same was true of Agnes. If their status as Franciscans had been legally formulated, then the sisters themselves might have been covered by the same oral approval that Pope Innocent III had given to Francis and his brothers in 1209. However, it seems that Innocent III had given Francis this oral approval primarily because he was impressed with Francis's preaching abilities.

No brother, including St. Francis, ever claimed that the 1209 privilege extended to Clare and her sisters. Indeed the brothers had the examples of the Cistercians and other male orders who had opened themselves up to women and, as a result, were overwhelmed with their pastoral needs. Attending to the needs of increasing numbers of women who wished to enter religious life often sidetracked monks from other more interesting, strategic, and lucrative apostolates. Women were commonly considered by religious men to be a burden.

While monastic men capped or completely prohibited the membership of women in their orders, pious women began to set up quasi-monastic structures protected by local bishops, rich patrons, or by their own economic ingenuity. After the Fourth Lateran Council, Pope Honorius III recognized the need to regularize these women. He assigned a budding canonist, Cardinal Hugolino, to this task. Hugolino wrote to Pope Honorius describing these monasteries: there are "many virgins and other women who desire to flee the pomp and wealth of this world. They build for themselves some small dwellings in which they may live, although their own nobility seems to promise them a prosperous situation in this world."

This all seemed good enough, but Cardinal Hugolino continues in his letter to outline the problems that these monastic institutions brought to the Church: "Although foundations are offered to you for this purpose by many people in the name of the Roman Church, certain persons do not hesitate to impede the salutary founding intentions of those women, wishing that the correction, institution, and destruction of these foundations be reserved for themselves."

In other words, monasteries that claimed allegiance to the Roman Church were being managed by laypeople and local bishops. This meant that the spiritual disciplines of the monasteries could be determined by local bishops and others whose spiritual ignorance, excess, or laxity could undermine a monastery's potential for offering their members a place where a truly spiritual life might be pursued. It also meant that patrons or local bishops could institute or dissolve monasteries at will, undermining the stability of the institution of religious life itself. Women who were in monasteries one day and on the streets without a home the next day did not bring credibility to the Roman form of religious life.

In the end, Cardinal Hugolino, who by 1228 had become Pope Gregory IX, insisted that Clare accept a generic form of life for women who did not have an official rule. He wrote these constitutions himself, basing them on the Rule of St. Benedict. He gave Clare little room for negotiation, but after a hunger strike and other behavior that no doubt undermined her credibility in the eyes of the pontiff, Clare obtained certain exceptions to these constitutions that gave her monastery the ability to follow her vision of a Franciscan lifestyle.

When Agnes of Prague entered and wished to associate herself with Clare, she did not join a highly organized monastic order with an approved rule written according to its founding charism. There was a well-established Benedictine monastery right next to her family's royal castle that she could have entered. This certainly would have been an appropriate choice for one of royal blood. Instead, Agnes entered a fledgling order whose brothers were loved by some and hated by others, and whose women were asserting their dependence upon brothers who did not wholeheartedly accept responsibilities for their pastoral and physical needs.

Agnes's decision created a public stir throughout all of Europe. The gossip concerned Agnes's "conversion and holy manner of life." People told stories about the Bohemian princess who declined an offer of marriage from the emperor himself in order to build and enter a monastery. Rumors about the kind of holy lifestyle that Agnes had embraced brought joy and encouragement, and also incredulous amazement to many in Europe.

The Legend of St. Agnes of Rome

Clare had never met Agnes. In fact, Clare and Agnes never met. However, Clare had a sister, Catherine, whom Francis had renamed "Agnes." Catherine had run away from home to join Clare even before Francis and his brothers had finished preparing the Monastery of San Damiano. At the time, Clare was living with a quasi-monastic community close to San Damiano called Sant'Angelo di Panzo. When the knights in the family heard that Catherine had escaped, they went to the humble and unfortified Monastery of Sant'Angelo, captured Catherine, and when she resisted their efforts to take her back home, beat her until she seemed lifeless. Perhaps too embarrassed to bring back into town a young woman ignobly beaten by men whose honor depended on providing her protection, they rode off, leaving Agnes for dead. After Clare had nursed her sister back to health, Francis accepted Catherine into the Franciscan movement and changed her name to "Agnes" after the Roman martyr, St. Agnes of Rome.

The Legend of St. Agnes of Rome was well known during the Middle Ages. The entire *Legend* was read on the feast and octave of St. Agnes celebrated from January 21 until January 28. A kind of "holy week for women," the feast of St. Agnes honored the virgin willing to forsake all other riches in order to stay true to Christ, her husband. In the end, Christ proved his fidelity to Agnes by protecting her from rape, but not from death itself. While rape spoiled virginity, death brought with it the promise and certainly of resurrection. How this must be reinterpreted for modern women according to contemporary sensibilities is another issue, but for medieval women, St. Agnes of Rome was perhaps the ultimate feminine Christ symbol. Women knew her *Legend* by heart. The Agnes *Legend* was one of the earliest Christian texts to be translated into vernacular languages. It was dramatized in town squares all over Europe.

Clare did not know Agnes of Prague, but she did know well *The Legend of St. Agnes of Rome.* What do you write to a royal woman who has built herself a Franciscan monastery in a far northern place where people speak a strange language and eat unknown foods? For Clare, the very name of her addressee provided the bridge to conversation.

The connection was obvious. Agnes of Rome had spurned the advances of a Roman dignitary in order to keep her virginity pure for Jesus Christ. In her letter to Agnes, Clare states that Agnes of Prague had spurned the opportunity of a legitimate marriage to the king of the world! But Clare's admiration does not stop there. Agnes of Prague did not only choose Christ over a rich, royal, earthly husband, she chose the Poor Christ. Her choice was not to enter a rich and established monastery but to accept a Franciscan lifestyle of "holiest poverty and physical want."

In this choice, Clare suggests that Agnes of Prague accepts "a nobler spouse." The irony makes one smile. Who could be "nobler" that Emperor Frederick II? Agnes of Rome makes the same claim in her *Legend*. The son of the Roman prefect who courts her might be noble, but she has already been claimed by one who is "nobler." One wonders how many men in the history of the West since *The Legend of St. Agnes* was written have had their ambitions stung by this classic line. The Agnes *Legend* asserts that it was Christ who protected Agnes's virginity. Clare assures Agnes that Jesus Christ will keep her virginity "always immaculate and inviolate."

Since San Damiano was not in the walls of Assisi, it was vulnerable to attack. A few Franciscan brothers lived at the monastery and cared for the needs of the sisters, but they, of course, did not bear arms. If the monastery was plundered by thugs, the sisters had little to protect them other than their poverty. Why rob a house if there is nothing to rob? One temptation the monastery could hold for wandering warlords or brigands was the virginity of the women themselves. Although fasting and other physical disciplines could compromise womanly beauty, women had little protection against those bent on rape. *The Legend of St. Agnes* provided hope and strength for vulnerable women.

We know, in fact, that Clare's monastery was attacked. During Clare's *Process of Canonization,* Sr. Francesca said under oath that the Saracens had broken into the cloister of the monastery. Clare, who was bedridden at the time, insisted that her sisters take her to the entrance of the refectory and bring with them the pyx where the Blessed Sacrament was kept. Throwing herself on the ground before the pyx, Clare prayed: "Lord, look upon these servants of yours, because I cannot protect them!" Her prayers were answered, and the Saracens left without harming the sisters or the monastery.

Clare takes verses 8–11 nearly verbatim from *The Legend of St. Agnes of Rome.* Here one can see how perfectly this *Legend* fits Clare's situation. Agnes has not really given up a crown, with its accompanying jewels. She has rather said "no" to a less worthy crown and chosen a better one. Agnes had become the "queen" of Jesus Christ himself.

Clare's Hymn to Poverty

Clare next begins to explain the path to this everlasting happiness promised in the salutation. Agnes, because of her Franciscan choice, has fallen in love with the "Poor Crucified"— the one who "endured the passion of the cross, rescuing us from the power of the prince of darkness, and reconciling us to God." This choice of God, this love affair that God has with us even in our poverty, is such a source of joy for Clare that she breaks out in poetry: "O blessed poverty," "O holy poverty," "O noble poverty!"

This is the poverty that when embraced provides the lover with eternal riches! This is the poverty that promises not only eternal glory, but also a happy life. This is the poverty that the Lord Jesus Christ chose over everything else.

While this is lovely poetry, Clare's agenda is not literature but catechesis. Agnes is far from Assisi. Clare hopes to give her the essence of what it means to attach herself to the spirit of St. Francis. Poverty for Clare is not merely an abstract ideal; it is the very foundation of her life as a religious woman.

From Poverty to Joy

In verses 18–30, Clare preaches as a typical medieval preacher. The great preacher Saint Anthony of Padua outlined his sermons in the same way. Clare weaves together various scripture passages demonstrating the need to embrace the Poor Christ in order to find joy. Many of these passages have a particular meaning in the jargon of the early Franciscan movement.

For instance the passage, "For foxes have dens, scripture says, and the birds of the sky have nests, but the Son of Man, who is Christ, has nowhere to lay his head," refers practically in the Franciscan sources to one's choice of housing. The choice to open with this text is pertinent. Agnes built her monastery between 1232–40. Clare's admonition to follow Christ by living in poor housing comes right in the midst of Agnes's building project!

The Lord Jesus Christ chose to appear "poor in this world." Throughout the Franciscan sources this phrase refers to overcoming the embarrassment of asking for alms. In asking for alms, one publicly admits one's poverty. One also admits that one is dependant upon the goodness of others for alms. One should not be ashamed of this choice because this "beggar poverty," according to Clare, was the very poverty chosen by Jesus Christ himself.

In embracing poverty, however, one does not proceed directly to eschatological joy. Clare is very aware that the one who embraces poverty will experience the contempt of the world—including the contempt of religious people. Perhaps the deepest sting in the Franciscan journey is not the hunger or the cold, or even the vulnerability, but that those who should honor one for embracing the Poor Christ do not. What the choice for Christ brings is not honor, but contempt.

Clare talks about "contempt of the world" at the very heart of her Rule: "When the Blessed Father [Francis] saw that we had no fear of poverty, hard work, trial, shame, or contempt of the world, but instead, regarded such things as great delights, moved by compassion he wrote a form of life for us." Note that this "contempt of the world" is an essential landmark at the beginning of the Franciscan life. The "contempt of the world" must be embraced in the Franciscan lifestyle, otherwise when one is treated like the poor person that one has chosen to become, one will become angry and upset. Anger, of course, is the very antithesis of joy. To be a joyful poor person, one must not only expect but also embrace the contempt of even good people.

In the Franciscan tradition, spiritual joy is not only a gift but also a spiritual discipline. It flows from the practice of constant prayer, which one needs in order to keep one's perspective especially when tempted to anger, and from purity of heart. Spiritual joy is a choice that one makes to celebrate the goodness of God. It is the decision to possess nothing other than God.

Spiritual joy is a gift, it is a decision, and it is a task. One practices spiritual joy and refrains from the embrace of anger. No doubt, while enjoying the romantic beginning of her Franciscan journey, Agnes did not clearly appreciate Clare's exhortation to embrace the contempt of the world with the choice of spiritual joy. Soon she would begin to understand.

Heaven Belongs to the Poor

Agnes should be filled with joy because she, like Jesus Christ, has embraced poverty. Clare takes the beatitude, "Blessed are the poor in spirit, for theirs is the kingdom of heaven" (Matt 5:3), literally. The only ones who are guaranteed heaven are the poor. Others might enter heaven, but, as Clare says: "a camel will be able to pass through the eye of a needle before a rich person ascends into the kingdom of heaven" (see Matt 19:24).

Why does Christ make this guarantee for the poor in spirit? Because the person who loves something temporal is not pure in love. The lover who loves something other than the beloved does not have a single-hearted love. The lover who is single-hearted in love will, like Jesus Christ, gladly give up everything in order to love the beloved. It is love that makes the sacrifice of poverty possible.

Agnes has stored up treasures in heaven "where neither rust consumes them, nor moth destroys them, and thieves do not dig them up and steal them." Earthly treasures have to be protected. They need to be guarded. The one who has riches has to insure them and protect them from thieves. There is a kind of violence that is inherent in the protection of one's goods. The poor person is not forced to make provisions for defense. Poverty brings joy because the worry of loss, of destruction, and of theft does not exist.

Because of Agnes's poverty, she is worthy to be called "sister, spouse, and mother" of Jesus Christ. Clare uses this expression twice in this letter in verse 12 and again in verse 24. Certainly Clare was familiar with Francis's *First Letter to the Faithful* written for those who wished to put his preaching into action. In this letter Francis says that faithful people are:

spouses when the faithful soul is joined by the Holy Spirit to our Lord Jesus Christ. We are *brothers* to him when we do the will of the Father who is in heaven. We are *mothers* when we carry him in our heart and body through a divine love and a pure and sincere conscience and give birth to him through a holy activity that must shine as an example before others.

Agnes, by her decision to embrace the Franciscan lifestyle, is the spouse who is joined to Jesus Christ, the sister who does the will of God, and the mother who carries Jesus and who gives birth to him in holy activity that encourages and inspires others. Since Agnes's entire life has now been defined according to her relationship with Jesus Christ, these intimate ties of sisterhood, spousal relationship, and motherhood to Jesus Christ define her spiritual dynamism.

In other words, the spirituality of a Franciscan is energized by the embrace of poverty. While Benedictine spirituality finds its primary challenge and energy in embracing the joys and sufferings associated with the love of Christ found within community life and prayer, Carmelite spirituality in embracing and fostering contemplative prayer, and Dominican spirituality in study and in the exercise of preaching, Franciscans are energized as Franciscans only insofar as they embrace the depths of poverty. In joining with the Poor Christ and in accepting poverty with its accompanying contempt of the world, Agnes becomes the spouse, sister, and mother of Jesus Christ.

Fighting naked with the naked enemy was another familiar slogan used to express poverty's advantage in the early Franciscan movement. Because the devil is smart enough to know that the person who is naked has the advantage, Christians who choose to fight without stripping themselves of their garments are at a decided disadvantage. Nakedness is not an end in itself, it is just a wise way to be in the world.

Entering the eschatological struggle without possessions is good spiritual sense.

We find in Clare not a kind of penurious poverty that demands hardship without love. For Clare, poverty is the response of a heart that is willing to sell everything to have the treasure. As long as one keeps looking directly at one's beloved, this selling is joy even if the whole world thinks that one is crazy! Franciscans do not choose poverty because they are seeking the contempt of the world, but because they are willing to suffer the contempt of the world in order to be with the person that they truly love. For Clare, poverty is a love affair.

The Sacred Exchange

The idea of a "sacred exchange," or if you'd like, "holy business deal," is an ancient one in Christian spirituality and well represented in the Franciscan movement. The theme of "holy exchange" is found in the Roman liturgy in both the Divine Office and in eucharistic texts.

In the thirteenth century, Vespers on the feast of the Purification of the Blessed Virgin Mary on February 2 included this text as its first antiphon: "O admirable exchange! The Creator of humankind assuming a living body, chose to be born of a Virgin; and, becoming human without seed, lavished on us his deity!" This very Greek sounding invitation to engage in the mystery of "God who became human so that we could become divine!" was a favorite antiphon of the Fathers of the Church and remained popular in the Western medieval Church.

The theology behind this antiphon was that Christ, who is by nature divine, took on human nature. Through Christ's resurrection human beings, who are of course human in nature, are raised with Christ and adopted as sons and daughters into the dynamism of the Trinity. This sacred exchange is, of course, advantageous for human beings.

Clare extends this concept of the "sacred exchange" to the choice of poverty. In coming to earth, Christ chose poverty. When Christians choose to live a life in union with Christ in poverty, they choose to live where the earthly Christ himself lived, and according to the beatitude, are guaranteed heaven. This heaven, according to Clare, is a happy, eternal life. The fruit of choosing Christ as one's sole beloved is simply and always, for Clare, joy.

Saying Goodbye

Having exhorted Agnes to the embrace of the Poor Christ, Clare had shared with her the essence of her religious life. Clare assures Agnes that she has written only because of Agnes's own desire for holiness. Her desire for Agnes's success in her newly chosen lifestyle comes from her prayer in the innermost heart, which can also be translated as womb or innermost being of Christ.

Clare's image of indwelling is a beautiful and common form of medieval prayer. In the Basilica of San Francesco in Assisi there is a double-paned stained-glass window in the Upper Church. On one side the Christ Child is held on the breast/lap/womb/heart of Mary. On the other side Francis is held in the same way on the breast/lap/womb/heart of Christ. When the Franciscan, St. Angelo of Foligno (ca. 1248–1309) went to Assisi and saw this window she was immediately transported into ecstasy. Angela says: "When I saw a stained-glass window depicting St. Francis being closely held by Christ, I heard him telling me: 'Thus I will hold you closely to me and much more closely than can be observed with the eyes of the body.'" Clare's image of begging Agnes to embrace poverty from the depths of the innermost heart of Christ reflects this same intimacy.

There is nothing flashy about the kind of intimate spirituality that Clare expresses here. It does not require elaborate explanations. Clare is simply placing herself in union, even using a physical image of closeness, with the one that she has chosen as her most intimate companion. Because of her poverty, this intimacy has no barriers. There is no temporal thing competing for Clare's attention.

Clare closes her letter by asking Agnes to pray for her and for her sisters. Clare never saw herself alone, but always in companionship with her sisters. One gets a sense that although the letter is addressed to Agnes from Clare, in reality it is addressed to Agnes and the sisters of Prague from Clare and the sisters of San Damiano in Assisi. Clare consistently uses the word "sisters" rather than "nuns." The title of her Rule, which was approved in 1253, refers to the Rule as the "Form of Life of the Poor Sisters." Clare embraced not having the established prestige of a "nun" as part of her poverty and joy.

Clare hopes that through the prayers of Agnes, she and her sisters may be able to merit the mercy of Jesus Christ so that they might meet someday in heaven and enjoy the everlasting vision. Clare and Agnes can hope to "merit" the kingdom of heaven not because of their disciplined virtues but because of the Gospel promise: "Blessed are the poor in spirit, for theirs is the kingdom of heaven" (Matt 5:3).

CONTEMPORARY RELEVANCE

Clare's First Letter and Contemporary Spirituality

While the mystics can inspire and challenge us, they cannot define our individual paths. Each Christian must in the end go before God and learn his or her own call and ultimate identity. As Christians, however, we do have companions who have taken the journey of love before us. Clare is a good guide, and as a good guide, she will inspire different people differently.

Clare is a radical lover. There is nothing pretentious about her. She is not known for her ecstatic flights, for her esoteric mystical feats, or for her great deeds. She was a simple woman from a noble family in Assisi. Apart from her embrace of the Franciscan life, contemporary scholars would find her of little interest. She lived, she entered a monastery, she wrote a rule—the first rule written by a woman that was approved by the Church, which was quite a feat—and she died.

What attracts many to Clare is not her poverty, but her love. Clare embraced Christ as her lover and was willing to give everything to follow and to be held by her beloved. Clare was a woman of liturgy and of contemplation. She is able to weave Scripture and legend together at will with poetic freedom. She prayed her office and spent hours alone in the innermost heart of Christ. She prayed for her sisters, and her prayers protected them.

As much as we are attracted to Clare for her simple intimacy with God and her fervent prayer, we cannot be true to Clare unless we understand that the root of this intimacy is not an abstract spiritual theory but a real physical poverty. This is not a poverty wherein one owns nothing but the community takes care of one, but an embrace of the poverty that the poor themselves have. This poverty subjects one to vulnerability, cold, hunger, and the contempt of the world.

If one does not embrace this poverty out of love, one can easily become sidetracked by dread over this prospect. Clare's poverty is not a political statement, it is not even a contemporary understanding of the preferential option for the poor. Rather it is a response of giving all for the sake of the one that one loves. It is a relational faith that God will take care of one if one takes care of the business of God.

Clare's Poverty and the Preferential Option for the Poor

Do Clare's poverty and her love for the Poor Christ connect in any way with the contemporary concern for the preferential option for the poor? Certainly. Although Clare's worldview of embracing Christ as her bridegroom is significantly different than the experience of most contemporary women, her concern for the poor was just as tender. The very first witness in Clare's *Process of Canonization*, her childhood neighbor, Sister Pacifica de Guelfuccio of Assisi, said that "Lady Clare very much loved the poor," and that "she willingly visited the poor." The seventeenth witness, Lady Bona, the sister of Sister Pacifica, testified that Clare used to give to the poor food that she was to have eaten. Lady Bona testified that many times she was the one who gave the poor this food from Clare. The twentieth witness, Joanni de Ventura, the house watchman for Clare's family, reiterated the testimony of Lady Bona: "She saved the food they were given to eat, put it aside, and then sent it to the poor."

Clare also deeply cared for her own sisters who suffered from the poverty of the monastery. In the *Process of Canonization*, Sister Benvenuta of Perugia said that Clare "cleaned the mattresses of the sick sisters with her own hands." She reports the comical story that "one time, while washing the feet of one of the serving sisters, Clare bent over, wishing to kiss her feet. That serving sister, pulling her foot away, accidentally hit the mouth of the blessed mother with her foot."

Sister Benvenuta follows this with a very tender image. At night, Clare went through the dormitory and covered the sisters from the cold. If a sister had a tunic that was more ragged than her own, Clare exchanged her tunic for the one worn by the other sister.

We can see, therefore, Clare's tenderness toward those who were truly poor and feel a kind of connection with our own desires to care for the poor. Yet, Clare's concern for the poor went beyond a preferential option for the poor. Clare chose to embrace a certain sort of poverty so that she might affect, within her movement of women, the very structures that imprisoned the poor. But here, we are getting ahead of our story.

Certainly in this first letter we are introduced to a woman who is a great lover of God. Agnes, however, is a new recruit who has not yet been tested in her choice of life. Soon she will receive a test that will shake the very foundations of her commitment. When this happens, Clare will need to flesh out even more fully the instructions of her first letter.

Questions for Reflection/Sharing

1. What brings you the most joy in life? Can you in any way relate to Clare's insistence that the embrace of poverty brings joy?

2. Is the ancient image of a religious woman's "marriage to Christ" useful for contemporary women? Is there still a need for the celibate vocation in the contemporary church community?

3. Have you experienced glimpses of the mystery of your own poverty becoming joy within your own life?

Clare's Second Letter to Agnes

INTRODUCTION

In order to assure its longevity as a charitable institution, the hospital that Agnes had founded in Prague needed to be heavily endowed. Agnes's monastery, on the other hand, was to follow the Franciscan ideal of living on what the Lord would give day by day.

Medieval monasteries and other religious institutions were endowed with cultivated fields, vineyards, woodlands, waterways, and roads. These properties provided revenues by which the monasteries survived. In the case of large monasteries, these landed revenues often took over entire villages. The people populating these villages frequently served as laborers of the monasteries.

With the rise of the money economy and the breaking down of the feudal structure in the early thirteenth century, common people began to struggle for greater freedom and self-determination. In order to safeguard their holdings, monasteries and other ecclesiastical institutions often needed to counter the desires of common people to move up in status, and thus obtain for themselves a more humane lifestyle.

With this background, one can understand why both Clare and Agnes were so insistent on keeping their monasteries free from landed endowments and from privileges that would give the sisters in their monasteries the legal right to trample over the rights of the poor. The choice to be poor for Clare and Agnes was the choice to share in the plight of the poor. Poverty for Clare and Agnes wasn't just an ideal, it was a choice for loving the poor and for not usurping their rights under the guise of religion.

Pope Gregory IX was understandably nervous about legitimizing monasteries without landed endowments. If a monastery fell on hard times, the Pope would be forced either to give it aid or to suffer the criticism of those who would see the poverty of the sisters. Having worked with many monasteries in Italy, Gregory IX knew firsthand that sisters in poor communities often lacked religious discipline and sometimes even ran away from their monasteries. Wanting to establish Agnes's monastery on a firm foundation, Gregory IX rejected Agnes's dream of an unendowed monastery. In a series of official papal letters he connected the hospital and the monastery so that the financial assets of the hospital would also benefit the sisters.

Seeing that her determination to live Francis's ideal of poverty was being compromised, Agnes wrote to Clare. Clare responded with her second letter to Agnes written sometime between the spring of 1235 and the winter of 1238. Using the words of St. Francis himself, Clare encouraged Agnes to be faithful to the Franciscan ideal even under papal pressure. Her Franciscan vocation could not be compromised even by the Pope himself. Although Agnes was to be respectful toward Gregory IX, she was not to follow his advice.

Clare's second letter is a masterpiece of early Franciscan literature. Its discernment, sense of vocational identity, and fidelity in regard to papal authority provide an example from the Catholic tradition of a respectful yet discerning way of disagreeing with legitimate authority. Not having institutional authority as a woman, Clare does not escape into mystical visions in order to legitimate her claims. Rather, Clare insists on the primacy of the experience of God's call as having the ultimate authority. When there is conflict between one's vocational calling and legitimate authority, one is to be respectful but unyielding in the following of God's call.

CLARE'S SECOND LETTER

(1) To the daughter of the King of kings, handmaid of the Lord of lords, most worthy spouse of Jesus Christ and therefore, very distinguished queen, the Lady Agnes, (2) Clare, useless and unworthy handmaid of the Poor Ladies, sends her greetings and the prayer that Agnes may always live in the utmost poverty.

(3) I thank the one who liberally bestows grace, from whom every best and perfect gift is believed to come, because he has adorned you with such a good reputation founded upon your virtues and has made you shine with the honors of so much perfection. (4) He did this so that once you have been made a diligent imitator of the Father who is perfect, you may deserve to be made perfect, so that his eyes may not see anything imperfect in you.

(5) This is that perfection with which the King will unite you to himself in marriage in heaven's bridal chamber where he sits in glory upon a throne adorned with stars, (6) because despising the heights of an

earthly kingdom and the less than worthy offers of an imperial marriage, (7) you have been made an imitator of most holy poverty, and in a spirit of great humility and the most ardent charity, you have clung to the footsteps of him with whom you have been worthy to be united in marriage.

(8) Moreover, since I know that you are laden with virtues, I shall refrain from saying too much as I do not wish to burden you with superfluous words, (9) even though to you no word of those that could be the source of some consolation for you seems superfluous. (10) But because one thing is necessary, I invoke this one thing and advise you, by the love of him to whom you have offered yourself as a holy and pleasing sacrifice, (11) to be mindful, like a second Rachel, of your founding purpose always seeing your beginning.

What you hold, may you continue to hold,
what you do, may you keep doing and not stop,
(12) but with swift pace, nimble step, and feet that do not stumble so that even your walking does not raise any dust,
(13) may you go forward tranquilly, joyfully, briskly, and cautiously along the path of happiness,
(14) trusting in no one and agreeing with no one because he might want to dissuade you from pursuing your founding purpose or might place a stumbling block in your way,
preventing you, in that perfection with which the Spirit of the Lord has called you, from fulfilling your vows to the Most High.

(15) Now concerning this, so that you may walk more tranquilly along the way of the Lord's commands,

follow the advice of our venerable father, our Brother Elias, minister general. (16) Prefer his advice to the advice of others and consider it more precious to you than any gift.

(17) Indeed, if someone tells you something else or suggests anything to you that may hinder your perfection and that seems contrary to your divine vocation, even though you must respect him, still, do not follow his advice;

(18) instead, poor virgin, embrace the Poor Christ.

(19) Now that you have made yourself contemptible in this world for his sake, look upon and follow the one who made himself contemptible for your sake. (20) Gaze upon, examine, contemplate, most noble queen, desiring to follow your spouse, who is more beautiful than the sons of humankind, and who for your salvation became the vilest of men, despised, struck, and flogged repeatedly over his entire body, dying while suffering the excruciating torments of the cross.

(21) If you suffer with him, you will reign with him, grieving with him, you will rejoice with him, dying with him on the cross of tribulation, you will possess mansions in heaven with him among the splendors of the saints,

(22) and your name will be recorded in the *Book of Life* and will bring you glory among men and women.

(23) This is why you may forever in eternity share the glory of the heavenly kingdom rather than what is earthly and transitory, eternal goods instead of those that perish, and why you will live forever and ever.

(24) Stay well, dearest sister and lady, for the sake of the Lord, your spouse; (25) and constantly remem-

ber me, as well as my sisters—for we rejoice in the good things of the Lord that he is accomplishing in you through his grace—in your devout prayers to the Lord. (26) Also, as often as possible, please remind your sisters to pray for us.

CONTEXT

I was sitting in the piazza of Assisi talking with a friend and eating a gelato, when a friend of a friend, a friar in his late twenties, joined us for some conversation. In the course of the conversation I learned that this friar had escaped the terror of a contemporary dictator and was currently studying for a European province of friars. Because American politicians had singled out the dictator in question as being particularly problematic, I asked the young friar if he felt that this was in fact the case. His response left me breathless. "The man killed my father when I was four years old."

Suddenly a casual talk about politics in the piazza became personal. When I recovered from the friar's frank statement, I asked about his vocation as a friar. Why, I wondered, had he chosen to become a friar rather than to join a rebel force or to engage in some sort of retaliation for the harm that had been done to him and to his family?

Again with confident frankness, the friar explained that his decision was a choice for peace. "Politics is dirty business," he said. "Peace happens only when people choose it. I decided to choose peace."

Politics cannot be kept out of religion. This is true particularly of Christianity. Since the God that Christians believe in became human and lived among us, this God who offered us a vision of life suffered death at the hands of religious and civil politicians. If even Jesus could not escape the "dirtiness" of politics, Christians should not be surprised when the complexities of politics spur them into action and also challenge their good works.

Christians live with a vision that the world could be different. Our belief in heaven, in a life of eternal peace, inspires our human desires to invite this peace into the present world. The young friar chose the Franciscan life because he believed in a world that could be peaceful. He believed that peace was a choice, and he paid the price of exile from his country in exchange for this vision of peace.

Discernment and Politics

As human beings we must discern our choices within the politics of our time. While the Holy Spirit does not force hearts to follow the directions of its movements, the Spirit is flexible, dancing around what refuses to be moved. As Christians following the Spirit's lead we know that there are no simple answers to complex political problems. We recognize that even the choice for peace is a political one. We know that the choices we make as Christians can bring us harm. We also know that the embrace of the Cross brings us new life and peace.

In the case of a dictator with the blood of a nation on his hands, discernment becomes a choice of peace and then of distance. One might choose peace, but then one must do what one can to distance oneself from the harm that a person with an evil intent might cause one. This discernment, although agonizing because of the exile it entails, is a relatively simple one. Discernment is much more difficult when there is conflict between people of good will. This is the situation that is being described in Clare's second letter to Agnes.

Clare states the purpose of her letter clearly in her salutation. Agnes is to "always live in the utmost poverty." This poverty, of course, is a political as well as a religious decision. Agnes's choice not to marry into royalty but rather to embrace the Franciscan life had political consequences that resounded all over Europe. Her personal decision for peace was supported by Gregory IX who did not want the royal family of Bohemia to be tied in marriage to Frederick II of Germany. Pope Gregory IX wanted to make sure that Bohemia's many knights would remain loyal to the papacy rather than join German forces warring against papal interests.

Gregory understood Agnes's choice as a political choice, and he supported her, in fact encouraged her, in this choice. If Agnes remained unmarried, the immediate threat of united Bohemian and German forces would be abated.

Agnes's Franciscan aspirations were certainly religious ones. Her desire was to fall radically in love with the Poor Christ. She wanted to learn to pray. She wanted to live peacefully, and she wanted to place her resources at the service of the poor in Prague. Having been educated in the ways of politics as a royal daughter, Agnes was also deeply aware that her choice to enter the Franciscan movement was political.

Thirteenth-Century Politics and Agnes's Choice

In northern Europe the sympathy toward the Franciscan life played itself out a little differently than in southern Europe. The politics of the north favored the idea of a poor church that would lead by means of spiritual inspiration, and rich rulers, who would lead in terms of worldly wealth and power. Politics would be driven by secular rulers with the balancing influence of a Church that was morally astute and distant from the politics of the world.

In the south, however, Frederick II was constantly threatening the papal territory in central Italy. The Italian people saw the Germans as foreign invaders, and they often experienced the papal forces as cruel and despotic. Italians sided one day with the pope and another with the emperor, trying to use them both to gain wider freedoms and a more prosperous lifestyle.

With this background, it is not difficult to understand why Agnes's royal family was so supportive of Agnes's vocational choice. Elizabeth of Hungary had just been canonized, and Frederick II had infinite praise for the Franciscan woman who had embraced poverty and had provided all with such inspiration for holiness. The Bohemian royal family did not yet have its saint, and it placed all its hopes in Agnes. The hospital that Agnes built was richly endowed not only with Agnes's dowry but also with monies from the royal family. If the Church could provide workers able to serve the poor, the royal family of Bohemia would provide the resources necessary to make this service possible.

Agnes begins her vocation, therefore, with both papal and royal support. Although this support was no doubt important to Agnes, gaining this support was not the ground of her vocational choice. Agnes did want to fall deeply in love with the Poor Christ. She believed in the dream of Francis. She wanted to embrace poverty with all of her heart because she saw it as a path to deep intimacy with God.

Franciscan "Perfection"

It is this intimacy with God that Clare refers to as "perfection." This perfection, however, is not some sort of bland spiritual ideal. Rather, this notion of perfection comes from the Gospel itself: "If you wish to be perfect, go, sell your possessions, and give the money to the poor, and you will have treasure in heaven; then come, follow me" (Matt 19:21).

This perfection is the first step of the Franciscan vocation. Reading the stories of early Franciscans, one finds people joining the order who give their possessions away and then embrace the poverty of the Franciscan family. Agnes has done this by giving away her royal dowry. She has established a hospital for the poor and the sick. She has sold her possessions and has literally given the money to the poor. Now she is free to follow the Lord in order to find her treasure.

It is not surprising, then, to have Clare immediately jump to the glories of Agnes's treasure: "This is that perfection with which the King will unite you to himself in marriage in heaven's bridal chamber where he sits in glory upon his starry throne." The line is reminiscent of an antiphon read in the Divine Office for the feast of the Assumption. Agnes's choice to sell everything and give it to the poor has given her the intimacy that Mary has with Christ. She will be intimately united to the one to whom she has given her heart.

We seldom think about marriage as being an economic deal, but in fact, it usually is. One of the first steps in marriage is the combination of the economic resources of two people. While certainly some economic independence between two people is healthy and good, ordinarily most of the couple's resources are combined and used for both the raising of children and the keeping of the household. The union of hearts, minds, and bodies is also the union of checkbooks.

The Sacred Exchange

The Franciscan sees marriage with Christ, or spiritual union with Christ, as an economic deal. In fact, it is a *sacrum commercium*—a sacred exchange, or, one might even say, a holy business deal. How does this deal take place? Matthew 19:21 tells us simply—go, sell, give all to the poor, and you will have treasure in heaven, then come and follow me.

The concept of the *sacrum commercium*—the holy business deal with God—is at once wholly practical and also deeply mystical. It is practical in that it is truly a business deal. One gives everything to God, and one receives everything from God. In the first letter we saw that Clare sees this sacred exchange as being greatly advantageous to human beings. Whatever we give to God, God will return a hundredfold. Making a holy business deal with God, therefore, is nothing to fear.

I remember when, as students attending a Jesuit university, we would at times during liturgies sing the *Suscipe* prayer of Ignatius of Loyola. The prayer bothered me, because I didn't know if I could really trust God with everything. "Take Lord, receive all my liberty. My memory, understanding, my entire will. Give me only your love and your grace, that's enough for me."

Frankly, I was counting. OK, I thought. I'll give the Lord my life, my health, my intelligence, my freedom, etc. What do I get back, God's love and grace? That's all good, I thought, but not very practical. I have a long life ahead of me. I don't want God to strike me down with some kind of sickness, some kind of disaster that will make me suffer for the next sixty years! I'll take the love and grace when I'm seventy or eighty and have fewer years of practical necessities to worry about. I remember watching the members of the guitar group sing with all their hearts, "Give me only your love and your grace." Perhaps a bit cynically, I wondered if they really were praying.

Clare's sense of the *sacrum commercium*, the holy business deal, is in a sense as practical as mine was, but is filled with hope rather than cynicism. For Clare, entering into a marriage with God is truly a business deal. It is, in a way, the real, practical sharing of a checkbook. But the deal is skewed. My fears were legitimate, but the reverse of the reality. There is one who is getting the lesser part—in fact, Clare reminds us from Scripture in her first letter, the imbalance is a hundred to one. What we give, we receive back a hundredfold.

With Clare's help, Ignatius's prayer makes more sense. "Your love and your grace" are not to be thought of as sweet consolation in prayer while the rest of life and health is greedily snatched away by a God who demands everything. Rather, "your love and your grace" include all the practical realities of food, clothing, shelter, relationships, health, and happiness that I was so afraid of losing. We are merely asked to give our one part in order to receive God's hundredfold. Now this is news worth celebrating! Clare celebrates the advantage of this holy business deal over and over again in her letters.

In the Franciscan tradition, the image of intimacy with God, then, is a very practical sort of reality. It is this intimacy, this trust that God will come through with the hundredfold, that makes every day of the Franciscan life so challenging and full of love. One understands God's love not only from spiritual consolations but also from the very practical gifts that God gives in the midst of everyday life. Because God is the ultimate, generous lover, one never has to fear that one will be cheated by love.

I once was in a conversation with a Franciscan sister who asked about the vow of poverty within my own community, the Franciscan Sisters of Joy. I explained to this sister that my community does not own any property and that we give whatever we did not need from our salaries directly to the poor. For me, this style of life has been a deep grace and a profound happiness. I, therefore, was a little taken back when instead of celebrating the joy of my vocation with me, the sister responded, "What about your retirement? You should be saving everything for retirement!"

In fact, our sisters do have retirement savings, but we do not save "everything" for retirement. The heaviness and worry of the sister's response caught me off guard. Certainly one must behave prudently in regard to financial matters. However, one's whole life cannot be dedicated solely to worry about retirement. Parents do not put their child's welfare or education on hold until after they have their nest egg completely established. Neither does the prudent family completely ignore the issues of retirement until the children are out of the house. Decisions regarding a limited income are made on the basis of love. Love has its consequences; it is also full of blessings.

Poverty for Clare is a way of perfection, an intimacy wherein one is completely cared for and loved both within this world and in the next. Poverty is a celebration of freedom, of love, and of grace. It is a practical path toward holiness.

Institutional Elements

Although we do not have Agnes's letters, Agnes no doubt wrote to Clare concerning the troubles that Gregory IX was causing her. When Agnes had set up the hospital in Prague, she had carefully separated the considerable endowment of the hospital from the monastery. The hospital, being a charitable institution, was to be heavily endowed. The monastery, being the place where Agnes was to live her Franciscan vocation, was to remain without an endowment.

In addition to Agnes's endowment, Agnes's mother, Queen Constance, and Agnes's brother, Přemysl, margrave of Moravia, increased the hospital's endowment. These donations were also set up specifically for the hospital, not for the monastery.

Gregory IX, however, was nervous about the legal situation that Agnes was creating. If, for some reason, the royal family would withdraw its daily support from Agnes's monastery, the Holy See would be left with a monastery full of noble and royal women in dire poverty. Such a situation would not reflect well on the papacy. Other religious institutions who during a time of crisis would have issues of their own would be forced to provide additional support for women who, if they had planned with less undiscerning zeal and with more fiscal prudence, would not be in such dire straits. From Gregory's perspective, Agnes's impracticality needed to be corrected.

On May 18, 1235, Gregory IX wrote a letter to Agnes and her sisters unilaterally conceding the Hospital of St. Francis with all its assets to the monastery. In this way, the hospital would fiscally be under the monastery, and its assets would benefit both the hospital and the monastery. Since the sisters of the monastery were truly poor, the assets set aside for the poor could also be used for the benefit of the sisters without causing scandal.

While seeming to address very practical financial issues, Gregory IX's letter contradicted Agnes's vision. Gregory is forcing Agnes to accept an endowment for her monastery. The acceptance of such an endowment would literally be, for Agnes, a taking back of the first step of her Franciscan vocation—go, sell all you have and give it to the poor. Agnes found herself in a difficult situation. She had given her dowry to God. Was she now to take it back?

Worse still, Gregory legally bound the hospital to the monastery. This meant that the sisters of the monastery would be the legal beneficiaries of the large sums of revenue from the landed properties given to the hospital not only by Agnes, but also by Agnes's mother and brother. Agnes was being asked not only to take back what she had given, but actually to usurp what her mother and her brother had given specifically to the poor of the hospital.

Finally, Gregory's policy legitimized not only the survival of the monastery but virtually insured its prosperity as well. The large hospital endowment was sure to bring in considerable income. Wealth corrupts, and Agnes's monastery would be forced to take the initial step of the Franciscan vocation over and over again—go, sell, give to the poor. The maturity of actually living the Franciscan way of life after the initial decision would never be obtained.

When Francis gave the money he stole from his father back to the bishop along with the clothes off of his back, he made an irrevocable choice. In disowning his father, Francis cut himself off from the wealth, prestige, and social connections that were his patrimony. Agnes had thought that she had followed the Gospel admonition of selling all and giving to the poor. She had endowed a hospital for the poor of Prague and left her own monastery without a guaranteed income. Gregory IX was threatening to undo this first step.

Perhaps hardest on Agnes's heart was the knowledge that a certain type of economy was needed in order to follow the Franciscan way of life. This type of poverty did not accept the type of landed endowments that brought in revenues on the backs of the poor. Agnes knew that her family supported her efforts. In becoming poor, she provided the less fortunate with a better way of life. The riches of the royal family now literally belonged to the poor. Agnes's action, in a sense, turned the economy upside down. The poor became rich, and a royal became poor.

The situation is perhaps seen more clearly by taking a look at a letter from Gregory IX that outlines the financial policy he established for Prague. One sees clearly the vast riches at stake and the undermining of Agnes's Franciscan vision. Gregory writes:

> Moreover, let whatever possessions and goods that same monastery and hospital might now possess as their own goods legally and canonically, or which you will in the future receive with God's help from a concession from popes, the generosity of kings or princes, an offering of the faithful, or in other just ways, remain firm and untouched for you and your successors. We have decided that these items under discussion ought to be clearly and specifically described as being that place, in which the aforesaid monastery is located, with that hospital and all its appurtenances; the estate of Hloubětín, with all the small estates pertaining thereto, namely Humenec and Hnidošice, the estate of Borotice and Dražetice, the estate of Rybník, with all its appurtenances, the estate of Rakšice, with all its appurtenances, and your other possessions, with fields, vineyards, lands, woods, properties held in usufruct, and pastures, with all other freedoms and their immunities regarding forest and field, waters and mills, and streets and paths.

Clare's Choice of Poverty

Clare understands Agnes's struggle. She had suffered the same heavy-handedness from Gregory IX who was eager to organize the many beguine-like monasteries in central and northern Italy. In order to move ahead with his program,

Gregory IX needed Clare's support. Yet, he had a problem. Francis himself had written to Clare telling her not to compromise the poverty of her monastery. Gregory IX, who had been a friend of Francis and had known him personally, needed to undermine Francis's authority on this issue just a bit without criticizing the vision of Francis himself. He writes to Clare and her sisters asking them to accept the fact that life cannot be lived in the past:

> We ask your community, exhort you in our Lord Jesus Christ, and command through apostolic documents that, just as you have received a Rule of Life from us, while walking and living in the Spirit, you forget the past and, with the Apostle, move on toward the future by striving after the better gifts.

In the end, Clare accepted the form of life that Gregory IX had written for her monastery only on the condition that her monastery remain without landed endowments. The Pope grudgingly gave in to this compromise, giving Clare her Privilege of Poverty on September 17, 1228. In his letter he first summarizes Clare's request: "For this reason, having sold everything and distributed it to the poor, you propose to have no possessions whatsoever, in every instance clinging to the footsteps of him, who was made poor for our sakes and is the Way, the Truth, and the Life."

Gregory gives Clare what she desires but only after placing a juridical spin on it. Clare is not exactly given the privilege of having "no possessions whatsoever," as she had asked, but rather is given the privilege not to be "compelled by anyone to receive possessions." This gives the Pope the ability to revisit the issue again at a future date. He writes: "Therefore, just as you have asked, we confirm with apostolic favor your proposition of most high poverty, granting to you by the authority of the present document that you cannot be compelled by anyone to receive possessions." The privilege wasn't exactly what Clare had asked, but it allowed her to follow the Franciscan life.

Once Clare received this Privilege, she protected it with all of her strength. Constantly being challenged to give up the precariousness of her monastery in preference to a more Benedictine-like institution that served the poor while maintaining strong fiscal viability, Clare held on to poverty as the core of her vocational identity.

In her process of canonization, Clare's sisters testified to Clare's determination not to give in on the issue of poverty. One of the sisters said of Clare: "She [Sister Benvenuta] also said that she [Clare] had an especially great love of poverty. Neither Pope Gregory nor the Bishop of Ostia could even make her consent to receive any possessions."

Another sister, Sister Pacifica said that:

> Clare particularly loved poverty, but she could never be persuaded to desire anything for herself, or to receive any possession for herself or the monastery. Asked how she knew this, she replied that she had seen and heard that the Lord Pope Gregory, of happy memory, wanted to give her many things and buy possessions for the monastery, but she would never consent.

The testimony of Sister Filippa supports the fear that Clare felt concerning the precariousness of the economic system chosen by the sisters of San Damiano: "She [Clare] could never be persuaded by the Pope or the Bishop of Ostia to receive any possessions. The Privilege of Poverty granted to her was honored with great reverence and kept well and with great diligence since she feared she might lose it."

Again one must remember that more is at stake for Clare in obtaining the Privilege of Poverty than simply an attachment to an ideal. Clare was not trying to play some kind of game of "I'm poorer than you are!" For Clare, poverty was associated with landed endowments. These landed endowments brought to Church institutions power, riches, and prestige that often took advantage of the labor of the poor. Clare's action turned this economic reality upside down. By literally joining the ranks of the poor, Clare and Agnes followed in the footsteps of Christ who chose poverty so that human beings might become rich. In doing so, they begin to create a world where the poor are given both nobility and the financial means to better their lives.

Clare's Advice

Since Clare personally understands Agnes's struggle, she is able to guide Agnes with a sure and ready hand. Agnes is to be like a second Rachel—a clear-sighted woman who remembers the founding purpose of her beginning. Clare tells Agnes, "Remember why you made this choice in the first place. Hold on to this."

Agnes is to hold on to what she already has. She is to keep doing what she is already doing. Moreover, she is to maintain her freedom in this choice without becoming sad or upset when she is not supported by papal authority. In this freedom, however, Agnes is to behave so that her walking "does not raise any dust." The image of dust in Franciscan literature symbolizes the worries and cares of the world. Agnes is to walk briskly, nimbly, and joyfully in her happiness, but she is to distance herself from the cares of the world. In other words, Clare tells Agnes to "do what you do, keep your spirit at peace, stay happy, and don't stir up trouble."

Clare follows this further with some of the most radical advice found in Franciscan literature. In this, one must remember that Clare as a woman is without institutional power within the Roman Church and therefore lacks the institutional channels by which she might protect the Franciscan feminine charism. Because of this, women throughout the ages have had to use alternative means such as the power of visions, influential friends, hunger strikes—which, by the way, Clare used at one point in order to obtain her Privilege of Poverty—in order to influence policies that directly impacted their lives.

Clare suggests two strategies to Agnes. First, she is simply to resist. She is neither to trust nor to agree with papal wisdom when it comes to the poverty that is at the root of her vocational identity. In suggesting this, Clare is on firm ground. It is St. Francis himself, recently canonized by Gregory IX, who gave Clare instructions to guide her in this very matter. In her Rule, Clare quotes directly from Francis's last will to her and the sisters of her monastery. In advising Agnes to respect, but not to follow papal advice, Clare is calling upon the authority and mandate that Saint Francis gave to her and to her sisters.

> I, Brother Francis, little one, wish to follow the life and poverty of our Most High Lord Jesus Christ and his Most Holy Mother and to persevere in this until the end. And I ask and advise you, my ladies, to always live in this most holy life and poverty. And guard yourselves assiduously so that you may never stray from this in any respect whatsoever neither because of the teaching nor because of the counsel of anyone.

Second, Clare advises Agnes to "follow the advice of our venerable father, our Brother Elias, minister general." Agnes is to "prefer his advice to the advice of others and consider it more precious to you than any gift." Clare sees and experiences herself as part of the Franciscan movement established by Francis. As such, her obedience, even though this is not established in law for Clare, is to the minister general of the Franciscan Order. If Agnes owes obedience to someone as a Franciscan woman, it would be to Elias, not to Gregory IX.

Many wonder about Clare's seeming support of Brother Elias in this letter. I'm not sure that Clare's support or lack of support for the person and agenda of Elias as minister general of the Franciscan Order at the time can really be discerned from Clare's words. Clare is offering Agnes what she needs—pastoral advice. Her recourse is to the words of Francis himself. Clare's position is based on a solid foundation in this regard. If further assistance is needed, Agnes must go to the minister general, to whom she has promised obedience, and treasure his counsel.

Embrace the Poor Christ

Clare understands that if Agnes does not follow the advice of Gregory IX that she will suffer consequences. In fact, Agnes's persistence will cost her the esteem of the Pope. How is she to endure this suffering?

Clare's advice is that Agnes should "embrace the Poor Christ." In order to save humankind, Jesus Christ became poor. He made himself contemptible in this world so that all might be saved. It is Agnes's turn now to embrace her lover who has endured and understands what it means to suffer contempt at the hands of another.

To enter into union with her spouse who wishes to unite himself to her in suffering, Agnes is to gaze upon Christ, examine him, contemplate him, and then follow him. Agnes is to love her beloved Christ even in profound suffering—the contempt of religious superiors toward one's vocational identity. Like Christ, Agnes is to suffer this contempt. With Christ, she is to find union in this contempt. United with Christ, she is to obtain the depths of true love with the one to whom she is promised.

The dynamic here is really rather simple. Suffering can break relationships or it can bring those who love each other into deeper, more mature relationships. If one is to move into this depth of relationship, one must choose during the suffering to gaze upon, examine, contemplate, and continue to follow one's beloved. This loving gaze, which was so easy during times of consolation and happiness, must now be chosen amid tears and sorrow. Instead of turning one's eyes away from love, Clare teaches Agnes to gaze on her beloved even in her suffering.

Agnes's spouse is more beautiful than any man, but Agnes is to gaze on him who was "despised, struck, and flogged repeatedly over his entire body, dying while suffering the excruciating torments of the cross." The scene is not a pretty one. If one truly examines it, one can hear, taste, see, feel, and smell the contempt. The contempt that Agnes is experiencing is, of course, small in comparison. Gazing upon what her beloved has suffered puts everything in perspective. More than that, it is the very means by which she is able to unite herself more closely to her beloved. Clare invites Agnes to see Gregory IX's contempt of her as a great joy. In being united with her beloved in suffering contempt, Agnes is actually beginning to look like the one whom she loves.

This spirituality, however, is not morbid but full of hope. Christ's resurrection assures the Christian that death, contempt, sorrow, and suffering are not the end but the beginning. If one suffers with Christ, one will reign with Christ. If one grieves with Christ, one will share in Christ's joy. If one dies with Christ on the cross of tribulation, one will share in all the splendors of heaven with the saints in glory. One gazes upon the cross, one suffers contempt and humiliation with the Lord only because the Lord alone is able to lead one through suffering, humiliation, and even death into the depths of loving union with God.

If one looks at the San Damiano cross, which Clare contemplated, one does not see a suffering Christ but rather a Christ who, although crucified, has his eyes cast in confident hope on the fidelity of his Father. Even while suffering contempt, one can experience the consolation of the glory of God.

A Good Business Deal

If Agnes stands firm in her choice of following the Poor Christ, what will she receive from the Lord? Is following Christ in contempt a good business deal? Is Christ a good and honest merchant?

Clare assures Agnes that Christ in fact can be trusted. In return for suffering contempt from the Pope, God will bestow upon Agnes glory that will be seen by men and women. In fact, in the life of Agnes we know that this is exactly what happened. Even though Agnes suffered papal contempt— although she prudently did her best to keep this to a minimum—the common people respected her as a symbol of fidelity and freedom. It was because of her poverty that Agnes was allowed to stay in Prague when the rest of the royal family was exiled. It was in Agnes's poverty that the poor in Prague were able to find comfort and to keep a member of the royal family among them.

Americans have a difficult time, perhaps, understanding how important to the common medieval man or woman this royal presence might be. Only a few years ago, I went to Prague and was introduced by a Czech sister to a poor woman who had a room in their convent. After the introduction, I was told by the sister in a whispered tone that "she was a member of the nobility." Royalty was more than bloodline, it was a pact with the common people. This pact, if those in power were good or even holy, provided security and protection for those who were poor. The good king and queen were a source of life for their people. Later in her life, Agnes's choice of poverty protected the poor and sick who came to her hospital, but it also allowed her to remain with her people in poverty while the rest of the royal family were forced to leave Prague.

Clare's second letter, therefore, ends appropriately with the *sacrum commercium*—the holy business deal. Agnes has given up power and riches but will receive heaven in exchange. She has given up clothes and jewels and earthly riches, but will obtain riches that do not perish.

Clare already in faith celebrates "the good things of the Lord that he is accomplishing in you through his grace." Convinced that Agnes's suffering will bring a kind of practical glory, a kind of powerful grace that can actually be effective among human beings, Clare asks that Agnes remember her in prayer.

CONTEMPORARY RELEVANCE

Clare's Second Letter and Contemporary Spirituality

No one wants to be poor these days. Rich people want to become richer. Poor people want to win the lottery. Young people often try to choose professional careers that will give them more monetary advantages for less work. Churches and religious institutions attempt to invest their money wisely in order to expand their programs and services.

Money is needed to do good works. If Church institutions are to pay fair wages to their employees and expand services to the poor, money is necessary. If religious congregations desire to institutionalize the good works of their members, endowments are needed. If families are to be supported, children fed, and tuition paid for, financial security must be a priority.

Given the practical need for money, perhaps Clare's insistence on both personal and corporate poverty is a medievalism that should be relegated to the archives. Gregory IX was an institutional man, skilled in law and versed in practicalities. Clare's stubbornness in regard to poverty did not help Gregory bring about institutional unity for women, nor does it, at first glance, seem to have moved women forward.

Why would women choose poverty when they are already victims of social and ecclesiastical prejudice? Other monastic women, such as the Benedictine Monastery of San Paolo delle Abbadesse, which Clare herself sought out for refuge, acquired riches, possessions, privileges, and power in order to protect its women from secular and ecclesiastical exploitation. Clare had the example of this monastery in her backyard. It was a good model, and it was working well. Why would Clare insist on the paradigm of corporate poverty even when the papacy gave her the legitimate means to move past her first zeal? Why would she suffer so much, choose to be despised by those with more power and experience, and endure the daily consequences and the stress of living a poor lifestyle? What did Clare see in the choice of poverty? Can the insights of her choice be applied to contemporary life?

The early thirteenth century was not completely unlike our own. The Fourth Lateran Council advocated widespread clerical and liturgical reform. The policies of Innocent III permitted greater freedom for the laity to express religious sentiment and to use their gifts of leadership. The money economy was expanding throughout Europe, and people who had once been slaves of the land now owned their own property and housing. Global trade and marketing were becoming facts of life, and global communications and travel were becoming more accessible.

In the midst of this newfound wealth and prosperity, real people were left behind. The misery of the sick was always present. The poor continued to labor under horrible conditions and were often exploited not only by nobles and merchants but also by the Church. People who fell upon ill fortune were exposed to impossible debts that would enslave them and their families.

Violence was everywhere. Merchant fought against knight for power. City fought against city for supremacy. Kingdom fought against kingdom; pope fought against emperor. The new power, the new money, the new prosperity was not bringing peace.

There seem to be two religious solutions to poverty as a social ill. The first is to use the resources that a religious institution has gained from being a part of the society in order to give back to the poor the resources that society has usurped. We are exhorted by the Gospel to feed the poor, clothe the naked, and to take care of the sick. To do these works of mercy, we need resources. Religious institutions have historically led the way and still, to a great extent, continue to lead the way in caring for the needs of the poor through the sharing of their resources.

Clare, however, had a different vision. Clare wanted to join the poor by literally and definitively giving the resources that she had as a noblewoman to the poor. In the eyes of Gregory, this was a foolhardy gesture. Institutions cannot endure without financial stability and longevity. Why would women want to dedicate their lives to a monastery that might not have the means to provide them with the very basic necessities of food and clothing? Was Clare violating the very basic principle of love for her sisters by her unrelenting and seemingly unintelligent insistence on institutional poverty?

Recently I was involved in a conversation that discussed what an institution might do with a large grant that was being courted. My colleagues wanted to set up studies and institutional mechanisms that would spend its energies on enlarging the initial grant. I found my own soul perplexed by this thinking. I wanted to give the monies as scholarships directly to exceptionally gifted poor students to train them as leaders. During the conversation, as I was perhaps more insistent than I should have been at the moment, a colleague turned to me and said: "Joan, if we do that, all the money will be gone." His comment stopped me short. "Of course," I thought. "And then we would be free again!" Obviously I was thinking like a Franciscan.

Let's for a minute, however, play out the possibility of giving the money away. The resources of the rich—in this case education—would now be given directly to the poor. Of the twenty students who would have received substantial scholarships, perhaps only two or three would persevere in their studies and return to serve the communities that they understand in a way that those of us who have not come directly from poverty do not. Statistically this is a very small return.

We have a sister in our community who, years before she joined us, had been an alcoholic and had lived on the street. After making a Nineteenth Annotation Retreat during her integration period, she discerned with the community that God was calling her to set up a Catholic Worker House. She uses her salary, which she earns by administrating another house for disabled adults, to pay rent to a slum landlord— $1500 per month for a slum flat. She takes in eight women from the streets who are in recovery. There is no endowment for this house. When she is unable to continue, the house will simply be rented to someone else, unless another group or person is able to continue her ministry. Perhaps one or two of the women will become well enough to do some sort of ministry of their own. Who knows? The point is that today women are being saved from danger by having a safe and healing home.

Wouldn't it be better to buy a large house, set up an endowment fund, and serve more women? Perhaps. The above model is based not on money and power but on resurrected hope. Jesus chose poverty so that we could share divine life. When the sister who began this house gives everything that she has away—and the rest of us help her—we are beginning the work of equalizing the world. The rich—those with education and employment—are becoming poor; and the poor have the resources—food, housing, education, healthcare— of the rich.

Clare did not spend her life criticizing religious institutions that worked out of the first model. In fact, both she and Francis sought help from the Benedictine monasteries surrounding Assisi who graciously cared for them. Francis received the little church of Saint Mary of the Angels from the Benedictines and told the friars never to leave the place. Clare received protection from the Benedictines who safeguarded her from the violence of the knights in her family who were infuriated by her decision to join the Franciscan movement.

What is essential is not how we live the Christian life but that we live the Christian life according to our vocation. No one, not even the pope himself, Clare insisted, has the right to interfere with a true vocation given by God. One must be who one truly is before God. As Francis used to say: "I am who I am before God, nothing more and nothing less." If one is clear in regard to one's vocational identity, then one can also appreciate and respect the vocational identity of another.

Clare is not talking about living a simple lifestyle, about being charitable toward the poor, or even about doing direct ministry with the poor. The poverty that Clare is speaking about is a radical economic choice to give money away directly to the poor without any strings attached. This Franciscan foolhardiness of Bernard, Francis, Clare and so many others can still be found today in Catholic Worker Houses and L'Arche communities.

The choice of those who could have had a comfortable lifestyle to share the lot of the poor is still a powerful symbol of the God who gave everything away so that we could share in divine glory. While all of us might look at Clare and admire her abandon, we must also honestly ask ourselves how God is calling us to respond to the plight of the poor. Our response must be discerned within the reality of our primary vocation.

Obviously a mother who has children to care for cannot give all her family's money away to the poor and put her children at risk. While Clare's example is a radical one, the theological foundation of her choice is a practical one. One must discern one's response within the reality of one's vocational call. Even if one suffers the misunderstanding of others in doing this, the freedom of living out who one truly is before God brings joy and peace. Giving "our all" is a very small price to pay for enduring happiness, eternal treasures, and true peace. It is good to do business with God.

Questions for Reflection/Sharing

1. How would you describe your own experience of discovering your vocational identity? What aspects of your vocational identity would you be unable to compromise?

2. Have you ever been scorned by good people because of a commitment that you in conscience could not compromise? How did you spirituality survive this contempt?

3. How would you describe your own personal commitment to the poor?

Clare's Third Letter to Agnes

INTRODUCTION

Most likely Clare wrote this letter in the summer of
1238. Through a series of interesting political maneuverings,
Agnes has obtained the Privilege of Poverty for her monastery from Gregory IX. Clare is happy to have a sister who is
as dedicated as she is to the pursuit of both personal and
communal poverty. She refers to Agnes in this letter as "God's
own helper."

Although Agnes was able to obtain the Privilege of Poverty
from Gregory IX, Gregory was not at all happy that another
monastery would be following the path of absolute poverty.
Gregory still hoped to unify the many monastic communities
of women living without official rules under the Rule of St.
Benedict and the constitutions that he himself had composed. Women who were trying to distinguish themselves
from the group were problematic for this unity.

Along with the Privilege of Poverty, therefore, Gregory
issued a decree mitigating the fasting requirements of Agnes's
monastery. No doubt the Pope thought that permission to
eat a wider variety of foods and the requirement to obey certain laws of fasting would present such a burden to the

brothers begging for Agnes's monastery that Agnes would
need to face the reality of an endowed monastery. Under the
new papal policies, the brothers would have to beg from the
poor and middle-class people surrounding Agnes's monastery specific kinds of food for the sisters. Concerned that
these new fasting laws were contrary to the instructions that
Francis himself had given to Clare, Agnes wrote to Clare asking for direction.

A masterpiece of Franciscan literature, Clare's third letter reminds Agnes not to get upset about anything other
than "the one thing necessary." Having the permission to live
without corporate property frees Agnes to live a Franciscan
lifestyle. One can always practice a stricter form of fasting,
but the privilege to live without landed endowments is key,
according to Clare, to the Franciscan vocation. Clare insists
that Agnes abandon her worry and care and live in the joy of
the Lord.

Francis did give Clare instructions concerning fasting.
Clare passes on these instructions to her Bohemian sister but
warns her not to compromise her health and spirit at the service of fasting. The colder Bohemian climate and the lack of
fasting foods grown in the Italian sun will require adjustments.

CLARE'S THIRD LETTER

(1) To Agnes, most venerable lady and sister in
Christ, deserving of love before all other mortals,
blood-sister of the illustrious king of Bohemia, but now
sister and spouse of the Most High King of the heavens,

(2) Clare, most humble and unworthy handmaid of Christ and servant of the Poor Ladies, sends her prayer for the joys of salvation in him who is the Author of Salvation and for everything better that can be desired.

(3) I am filled with such great joy about your well-being, your happiness, and your favorable successes through which, I understand, you are thriving on the journey you have begun to obtain the reward of heaven; (4) and I breathe again in the Lord with elation equal to my knowledge and belief that you are supplying in wonderful ways what is lacking both in me and in the other sisters who are following in the footsteps of the poor and humble Jesus Christ.

(5) I am indeed able to rejoice, and there is no one who could separate me from such great joy, (6) since I already possess what under heaven I have yearned for, and I see that you, supported by some kind of wonderful claim on the wisdom that comes from God's own mouth, are formidably and extraordinarily undermining the stratagems of the cunning enemy, the pride that destroys human nature, and the vanity that beguiles human hearts. (7) I see, too, that you are embracing with humility, the virtue of faith, and the arms of poverty the incomparable treasure that lies hidden in the field of the world and in the hearts of human beings, where it is purchased by the One by whom all things were made from nothing. (8) And, to use as my own the words of the apostle himself, I consider you someone who is God's own helper and who supports the drooping limbs of his ineffable body.

(9) Who, then, would tell me not to rejoice about such great and marvelous joys? (10) That is why you,

too, dearest, must always rejoice in the Lord, (11) and not let bitterness and confusion envelop you, O Lady most beloved in Christ, joy of the angels, and crown of your sisters. (12) Place your mind in the mirror of eternity; place your soul in the splendor of glory; (13) place your heart in the figure of the divine substance; and, through contemplation, transform your entire being into the image of the Divine One himself, (14) so that you, yourself, may also experience what his friends experience when they taste the hidden sweetness that God alone has kept from the beginning for those who love him.

(15) And completely ignoring all those who in this deceitful and turbulent world ensnare their blind lovers, you might totally love him who gave himself totally out of love for you, (16) whose beauty the sun and moon admire, and whose rewards, in both their preciousness and magnitude, are without end. (17) I am speaking about the Son of the Most High, to whom the Virgin gave birth and, after whose birth, she remained a virgin. (18) May you cling to his most sweet Mother, who gave birth to the kind of Son whom the heavens could not contain, (19) and yet, she carried him in the tiny enclosure of her sacred womb, and held him on her young girl's lap.

(20) Who would not abhor the treachery of the enemy of humanity who, by means of the pride that results from fleeting and false glories, compels that which is greater than heaven to return to nothingness? (21) See, it is already clear that the soul of a faithful person, the most worthy of God's creations through the grace of God, is greater than heaven, (22) since the heavens and the rest of creation together cannot contain their Creator and only the soul of a faithful person is his dwelling place and

throne and this is possible only through the charity that the wicked lack. (23) For the Truth says: The one who loves me, will be loved by my Father, and I shall love him and we shall come to him and make our dwelling place with him.

(24) So, just as the glorious Virgin of virgins carried him physically, (25) so, you too, following in her footsteps especially those of humility and poverty, can without any doubt, always carry him spiritually in your chaste and virginal body, (26) containing him by whom both you and all things are contained, and possessing that which, even when compared with the other transitory possessions of this world, you will possess more securely. (27) Regarding this, some kings and queens of this world are deceived; (28) even though in their pride they have climbed all the way up to the sky, and their heads have touched the clouds, in the end they are destroyed like a pile of dung.

(29) Now, I thought that I should respond to your charity about the things that you have asked me to clarify for you; (30) namely, what were the feasts—and I imagine that you have perhaps figured this out to some extent—that our most glorious father, Saint Francis, urged us to celebrate in a special way with different kinds of foods. (31) Indeed, your prudence knows that, with the exception of the weak and the sick, for whom he advised and authorized us to use every possible discretion with respect to any foods whatsoever, (32) none of us who are healthy and strong ought to eat anything other than Lenten fare, on both ordinary days and feast days, fasting every day (33) except on Sundays and on the Lord's Nativity, when we ought to eat twice a day.

(34) And, on Thursdays in Ordinary Time, fasting should reflect the personal decision of each sister, so that whoever might not wish to fast would not be obligated to do so. (35) All the same, those of us who are healthy fast every day except Sundays and Christmas. (36) Certainly, during the entire Easter week, as Blessed Francis states in what he has written, and on the feasts of holy Mary and the holy apostles, we are also not obliged to fast, unless these feasts should fall on a Friday; (37) and, as has already been said, we who are healthy and strong always eat Lenten fare.

(38) But because neither is our flesh the flesh of bronze, nor our strength the strength of stone, (39) but instead, we are frail and prone to every bodily weakness, (40) I am asking and begging in the Lord that you be restrained wisely, dearest one, and discreetly from the indiscreet and impossibly severe fasting that I know you have imposed upon yourself, (41) so that living, you might profess the Lord, and might return to the Lord your reasonable worship and your sacrifice always seasoned with salt.

(42) Stay well always in the Lord, just as I very much desire to stay well, and be sure to remember both me and my sisters in your holy prayers.

CONTEXT

Although not much time had elapsed since Clare had written her second letter, much had happened in Agnes's

Bohemian monastery. Gregory IX had hoped to set up the royal monastery in Prague as a heavily endowed institution. It was to possess many estates with their fields, vineyards, lands, woods, properties held in usufruct—meaning that although these properties belonged to others, any income that these properties produced would go to the monastery—pastures, forests, waters, mills, streets, and paths. In addition, Gregory wanted to protect the monastery from the payment of any sort of taxes or tithes: "Let no one presume to demand or exact from you a tithe from your fields that you cultivate for your own use, from which no one has yet taken a collection, or from the food for your animals."

Beyond this wealth and all of these exemptions, Gregory IX obliged the local bishop to donate to the monastery from the resources of the people.

> Let no one dare to exact anything from you under the pretext of custom or in any other way for the consecration of your altars or church, for making the holy oil or any type of ecclesiastical sacramental, but let the diocesan bishop freely pay for all these things for you by our authority.

Gregory's idea of a stable monastery for women is clear. It is to be heavily endowed with property that will bring in substantial revenue. This revenue is to provide products such as grains, wines, oil, and wood for the needs of the monastery. The monastery is not obliged to provide help to the local people, although in the spirit of the Benedictine Rule, this help certainly would be given and would, most probably, be substantial. This aid to the poor, however, is not formulated explicitly in Gregory's legislation, as the exemptions are, but depends upon the sense of justice of the sisters of the monastery. In addition, the local bishop is to provide from the resources of the people anything that the monastery might need for its sacramental functions.

Certainly Gregory IX understood that Agnes's royal family supported her and would contribute great wealth to Agnes's hospital and monastery. Her brother and her mother had already given large endowments to the hospital. Agnes's monastery would be a wealthy institution worthy of her royal status. It would also be an institution that would bring glory to the Roman Church.

We have seen in the second letter that Agnes became very concerned that her vocational identity was being undermined by Gregory's maneuverings. She wrote to Clare, and Clare encouraged her to hold her ground and to rely on Elias for advice and support. Agnes did speak with Elias. She also enlisted the aid of another person—her brother, King Wenceslaus I.

King Wenceslaus I

It seems that King Wenceslaus was very close to his sister and, like the rest of Agnes's family, completely supported her Franciscan aspirations. Being informed of Gregory IX's intentions, Wenceslaus wrote Gregory IX a cordial, but frank letter asking the Pope to listen to the request of his sister. One can hardly help but smile at the diplomacy of the letter. The letter has a friendly beginning.

> First, I return abundant thanks to your Most Excellent Sanctity for the fact that you never stop bestowing your kind affection on your very dear daughter and my beloved sister, Lady Agnes, in regard to her Order of Poor Ladies. She herself bears witness to the fact that she never recalls having offered any prayers to Your Sanctity whose desired effect she

did not soon obtain from your paternity. Hence, because of this truth your kindness draws me, with all my strength, which rests in my kingdom, family, in-laws, and friends alike, to itself and to the whole Roman Curia in all devotion.

It should be remembered that Gregory IX desperately needed the support of King Wenceslaus I. The German emperor, Frederick II, was trying to usurp the papal territories in central Italy. It was essential that any aid that Bohemia might give to the struggle would support the papacy rather than the Germans. Wenceslaus promises Gregory that he has his unconditional support: "After lengthy deliberation, I solemnly vow and promise to God that from this action I will sincerely wish to be always more ready and available for you and the Holy Roman Church in every necessity or opportunity, both public and private."

Although he is careful not to make papal approval of Agnes's desires a condition of his continued temporal support of Gregory IX, Wenceslaus I does make a subtle threat. His enthusiasm and readiness to support Gregory IX's agenda would be dampened if Gregory does not listen and respond favorably to Agnes's request.

This shall be particularly true if you will have decided with your customary kindness that the petitions of your above-mentioned special daughter and my most-beloved blood sister, which she herself has decided to offer to you now, ought to be admitted into the chapel of your kind hearing, knowing this to be sure and in every way established that, since you give satisfaction to her prayers, which without doubt are pleasing to God because they also come from Him, you receive me, as I have said, with all my power under your power, which is worthy in every respect.

Agnes Receives the Privilege of Poverty

Apparently the intervention of King Wenceslaus changed the Pope's mind. On April 14, 1237, Gregory IX dissolved the monastery's legal tie with the hospital and established it as an independent, unendowed institution just as Agnes had done in the first place. The endowments given to the hospital by Agnes, her mother, and her brother were placed under the authority of the Apostolic See. The brothers of the hospital, most probably because Agnes was staunchly opposed to the concept of Franciscans possessing propertied endowments, were given the Rule of St. Augustine and were placed under the supervision of the Dominicans.

Exactly one year later on April 15, 1238, Agnes received the Privilege of Poverty for her monastery from Gregory IX. The legal formulation of this privilege is the same as that given to Clare's monastery of San Damiano. Gregory, however, was not at all happy about Agnes's political victory. While giving her the legal document that she desired, Gregory would make further attempts to undermine her ability to live according to her desires.

The Request for a Franciscan Form of Life

The dynamic here, however, is not of a sexist pope who spent energy trying to undermine the efforts of good women. Gregory IX spent much of his papacy helping women's monasteries and even donated to them out of his personal resources. The problem was that Gregory's vision was essentially a Benedictine vision, while Agnes and Clare desired to live as Franciscans.

Agnes wanted to live under a Franciscan Rule and under constitutions based on the instructions that Francis had given to Clare. Less than one month after issuing the Privilege of Poverty for Agnes's monastery, Gregory denied this request. In his letter, Gregory IX insists that the form of life that St. Francis had given to Clare was merely "infants' milk." Concerning the Monastery of San Damiano, Gregory states: "Blessed Francis then gave to them a formula of life, seeing that a draught of milk, rather than solid food, was suitable for those who were like newborns." In contrast, Gregory insists that the constitutions that he had written were juridically mature and provided solid food for a truly religious life.

Gregory IX's notion that Francis's vision for the sisters associated with Clare was immature struck a dissonant chord with Clare. In fact, Clare will eventually put the issue at the very center of her Rule. Clare's claim is that it was not immaturity that inspired Francis but maturity: "When the Blessed Father saw we had no fear of poverty, hard work, trial, shame or contempt of the world, but instead, regarded such things as great delights, moved by compassion he wrote a form of life for us."

Gregory cites four reasons why he cannot accept Agnes's proposal for a specifically Franciscan Rule and constitutions. First, Clare and her sisters "solemnly professed the aforementioned Rule, which was composed with watchful zeal, accepted by St. Francis, and also, a little later, confirmed by our predecessor Pope Honorius of happy memory who, at our request, conceded a privilege of exemption to them." Both Francis and Clare had accepted the constitutions that Gregory had written for the Monastery of San Damiano. Gregory honored the special charism of Clare's monastery, to live without propertied endowments that would guarantee income to the monastery, by a papal exemption. Gregory's vision was clear. He wanted to unify beguine-like women's monasteries under the Rule of St. Benedict and his own constitutions. If the women in these monasteries wanted various exceptions to this, they could ask for a papal exemption. San Damiano asked for and received the Privilege of Poverty, as did Agnes's monastery.

To Gregory, the above seemed like a win-win situation. Gregory was able to obtain his goal—the juridical ordering of beguine-like women under the Benedictine Rule and his own constitutions. Clare and Agnes were also able to have their primary desire—the ability to live without landed endowments that would provide a regular income to their respective monasteries.

The second reason Gregory IX claimed that he could not grant Agnes's request for a specifically Franciscan Rule was because the sisters of San Damiano had put aside Francis's form of life and had professed the Rule of St. Benedict according to Gregory's constitutions. Gregory engages here in solid canonical argument. Sisters cannot be forced to live under a rule that they had not professed.

Third, and obviously this is Gregory's deepest concern, the uniformity of the Order of Poor Sisters that he had created is threatened by Agnes's request for independence. Gregory's union is established on a common rule and constitutions. He is quite happy to give the various monasteries privileges and exemptions according to their needs. However, if he deviates from the common rule and constitutions, the unity of his order collapses: "Since the Rule was established such that it is uniformly observed everywhere by all those professing it, it would be possible for serious and insupportable controversy to arise from a presumption of the opposite."

Gregory's fourth reason follows naturally. He imagines that the many small monasteries of beguine-like women that he has juridically organized will again fall prey to disorder. This

disorder would lead to a lack of discipline within the monasteries themselves and to a possible exodus of sisters from the
monasteries. This would bring scandal to the people of God.

With the above letter, Gregory sends Agnes another copy
of his own constitutions reminding her that through "happy
perseverance" her sisters may be able to grow "through the example and imitation of those who have served the Lord without complaint." Gregory's decision is definitive. Agnes did
not press the issue of a Franciscan rule again during his reign.

If Gregory won the battle in regard to the issuance of the
Franciscan Rule and a specific constitution for monasteries
associated with San Damiano, it should not be forgotten that
he did, under political duress, issue the Privilege of Poverty
for Agnes's monastery. He was not at all happy about this
situation, and seems to be particularly frustrated not only with
Agnes but also with Elias, the Franciscan minister general.

> We command your devotion and obedience in our Lord Jesus
> Christ, enjoining upon you for the remission of your sins that
> you consider what has been written above with careful medi-
> tation and prudently notice that, whatever might be suggested
> to you by someone who may be acting out of enthusiasm rather
> than intelligence, you ought to hold as most important in
> your affections what is able to be pleasing to God, acceptable
> to us, and wholesome for you and your companions. Thus
> with the merciful aid of the Redeemer, put aside every excuse
> and diligently observe the aforesaid Rule, making sure, also,
> that it is observed by your sisters.

Fasting and the Privilege of Poverty

With the Privilege of Poverty, the refusal of Agnes's request for a Franciscan Rule and constitutions, and the copy
of his own constitutions reissued for Agnes's monastery,

Gregory sent one more papal letter. This letter had to do with the mitigation of fasting practices in Agnes's monastery. It should be remembered that fasting and disciplined fasting laws were core to religious observance. Just as one would not have eaten meat on Fridays in a good Catholic home in the 1950s, so too, in medieval monasteries fasting practices signaled pious observance.

The northern kingdom of Bohemia did not enjoy the sun-kissed products of the Italian fields. Rules concerning fasting that were written in Italy were difficult to follow in Bohemia.

One month after issuing the Privilege of Poverty, a dispensation from certain fasting requirements was presented to the Prague monastery. The dispensation was a substantial one, with the monastery adding milk products and eggs to their diet on ninety-one days during the year. While this addition does not seem substantial to contemporaries, milk products and eggs were not considered fasting foods. Fasting foods included water, bread, salt, raw vegetables, fruits, nuts, oil, wine, pulmenta—which signified cooked foods, namely legumes, cake, gruel—and fish. Non-fasting foods included milk, milk products, eggs, fat, and meat.

One could go on to configure the complexities of trying to prepare supper for the sisters of Prague, but put simply, the problem was that Gregory's mitigations cut deeply into the ability of Agnes's monastery to live the Privilege of Poverty. In order for the Privilege of Poverty to work, the Franciscan brothers who lived in a small cloister attached to Agnes's monastery had to beg daily for food both for themselves and the sisters. Although it can be assumed that the royals helped with this burden, the friars also no doubt begged from the many poor people and small merchants who surrounded the monastery. Eggs and milk products required animals and were precious medieval commodities. Feeding an entire monastery of women eggs and cheese for dinner would place the table of Agnes's monastery above many of the tables of Prague's poor.

Clare's Rejoicing

Obviously Agnes had much to write to Clare. She no doubt shared her happiness in regard to obtaining from Gregory IX the Privilege of Poverty for her monastery. She expressed her terrible disappointment in not being able to move forward with the prospect of living under a Franciscan Rule and Franciscan constitutions. She asked for specific information on Francis's instructions to Clare's monastery regarding fasting.

Clare does not enter into Agnes's angst regarding the many concerns of Gregory's rejection of a specifically Franciscan Rule and constitutions and his new fasting prescriptions. Rather, Clare focuses on the fact that Agnes has obtained the Privilege of Poverty. As long as Agnes has this particular exemption, she is able to live a Franciscan lifestyle. Even if this lifestyle is not recognized in law, she can live her daily life in peace.

The first part of Clare's third letter, therefore, is all about rejoicing. Clare rejoices because Agnes is embracing "with humility, the virtue of faith, and the arms of poverty the incomparable treasure that lies hidden in the field of the world and the hearts of human beings." Agnes, like Mary holding the crucified Christ, is "God's own helper," and she herself is supporting "the drooping limbs of Christ's ineffable body."

Given such a great joy, why would Agnes give in to sadness? It's not legalities that are important, but the ability to live one's life according to one's vocation. Once one has obtained the freedom to live according to God's call, one possesses everything. All other issues are peripheral.

Agnes, then, "must always rejoice in the Lord," and let go of all bitterness and confusion. But how is Agnes to escape the frustration that she feels? How is she not to become embittered by the disdain of a pope who was willing to support her dream when it suited his political advantage, but belittles her calling and her person for the sake of a generic ideal of unity that fails to bring life to Agnes's heart? How can she forgive words that demean the guidance of Francis?

Clare understands that Agnes has reached a critical moment in her conversion. One expects that a religious person would be attentive and solicitous to the needs and desires of another religious person. In fact, Gregory IX was solicitous to the needs of the many women who needed guidance, direction, and financial stability. He was well aware of the fact that most of the friars, who were becoming more and more engaged in papal politics and important offices, were more attracted to the adventure of the missions and the prestige of papal and royal positions than they were to begging for nuns who had refused their own dowries.

Clare does not blame Agnes for her persistent stubbornness in regard to establishing the legal foundations of her form of life. In fact, Clare shared Agnes's stubbornness. On the other hand, it is also not difficult to understand Gregory's dilemma. What would have happened if Agnes had simply accepted Gregory's vision for her monastery?

Sisters who consumed milk, dairy products, and eggs would have needed some sort of pasture and/or farmland to support such luxuries for a large monastery over the long term. In Agnes's case, perhaps the royal family could have provided such commodities for the monastery, but such a concession would have placed the monastic table above the table of the poor.

Even more dangerous, from a charismatic perspective, is Gregory IX's vision for a legislatively generic form of religious life. As religious women, Clare and Agnes were fully aware of the Spirit's freedom. While religious institutions have successfully regulated many things, a religious vocation is, by definition, prophetic. As such, a religious charism is dangerous because it, at times, is called to prophesy against the corruptions found within the Church itself. The prophet's life is a life in love with God alone. Although one makes vows within a congregation and according to a rule and constitution, the essence of the vocation is availability to the Spirit of God. Laws cannot always successfully legislate the movements of this Spirit. Religious life, while respecting and submitting to the guidance of the Church, does not, in fact, belong to the juridical arm of the Church. It is a charismatic vocation.

In insisting that religious life is a charismatic vocation, one does not throw the discipline and practices of religious life to the wind. In responding to Agnes's angst, Clare does so as a mature religious woman. Wrath and anger against Gregory IX will not move the Franciscan agenda forward. There is a time for action and a time for waiting. Gregory has closed the door to the issue. Agnes has her Privilege of Poverty; now she must remain quiet and wait.

Eschatological Prayer

There is a story told about the Brazilian bishop, Dom Helder Camera. A sister once asked him, "How can you live in happiness when you know that there are people who want to kill you; when you know that there is a price on your head?" Dom Helder replied, "I have learned to listen to the angels sing."

There is perhaps nothing more painful than being at loggerheads with another, unable to negotiate, unable to compromise, and unable to make peace. Agnes finds herself in this position with the Pope himself. Clare, because Agnes has obtained the Privilege of Poverty for her monastery, insists that Agnes's situation is different than it was in her second letter. Clare does not suggest that Agnes further petition the minister general at this time or engage in other political activity. Rather, Clare suggests that Agnes change the situation by changing herself.

How is she to do this? Clare offers Agnes simple, but profound instructions. In her prayer Agnes is to place herself in the brightness of eternity. She is to place herself within the eucharistic presence. In doing this, she will find peace.

I had the privilege of spending time with a Franciscan sister, Sr. Margaret Halaska, before she died. Margaret is the only person that I know of who has actually had the courage to beg the Lord to give her the gift of poverty. She received this poverty as a brain tumor, as isolation from her own Franciscan community—as she was placed in a psychiatric nursing ward that did not belong to her community, and as a slow mental and physical disintegration. I met Margaret only a year before she died. During that year, I visited her almost daily. After I helped her eat supper and get ready for bed, all of which took many hours, she would want to pray together. We'd start to pray, and then she would become silent. Wondering if she were asleep, I'd ask her what she was praying about. She responded simply, "Oh I just go to God's throne and tell Mary all that the world needs." The first few times I thought to myself, "This is the sweet prayer of an old nun." But Margaret kept asking me to pray with her, and this was her simple prayer. Nearly every night for a year Margaret took me before the glory of God in heaven. As Dom Helder said, "I learned to listen to the angels sing."

Clare sees that Agnes is upset about many things. She has a right to be. But persisting in being upset, even though Agnes has the right to be upset, does not give one joy. Clare suggests that Agnes should completely ignore "all those who in this deceitful and turbulent world ensnare their blind lovers," and love God totally, "who gave himself totally out of love for you!"

Clare then adds advice very familiar to the prayer that my Franciscan friend, Margaret, also described. Clare suggests that Agnes "cling to his most sweet Mother, who gave birth to the kind of Son whom the heavens could not contain." If one becomes overwhelmed before the throne of God, before God's glory, one needs simply to find Mary, who is also there, and to cling to her.

Becoming Like Mary

For a religious woman, clinging to Mary, who is found worshiping before the throne of God, has a double dynamic. First, if one is bored, overwhelmed or lost in light before the throne of God, one can cling to Mary and find solace there. Second, being with Mary helps one understand more clearly the radiant glory of one's own soul. The divine glory that one experiences before the throne of God is already living and active, burning in the glory of one's innermost being.

Clare says: "See, it is already clear that the soul of a faithful person, the most worthy of God's creations through the grace of God, is greater than heaven." Why greater? Because the heavens and all of creation cannot contain their Creator, but Christ has promised that "those who love me will keep my word, and my Father will love them, and we will come to them and make our home with them" (John 14:23).

In placing ourselves before God's glory we first feel awkward, even bored. If we are able to persevere in this prayer, we begin to experience the depths of God's glory and find ourselves afraid to stay. By clinging to Mary, who is before the throne of God's glory, we learn to stay in the light of glory. We also begin to understand the glory and wonder of our own being.

The fruit of this eschatological prayer is perhaps best illustrated in Clare's own life. When she was on her deathbed, Clare exclaimed: "Blessed are you, O Lord, for having created me!" There is no false humility in Clare that prompts her to devalue the beauty of her own soul. Clare understands that her soul radiates the glory of God. The union between God and Clare is filled with radiant beauty and glory. She sees clearly the beauty of her own soul by resting in prayer before the glory of God. Like Mary, Clare holds the glory of trinitarian light within her.

Back to Fasting

Gregory IX's fasting mitigation for Agnes's monastery does not necessarily undermine the Privilege of Poverty. One can always choose to live a stricter religious life than the one regulated. Gregory does not order the sisters to follow the new regulations. Becoming obsessed with law will undermine Agnes's happiness. Agnes needs to "place her mind in the mirror of eternity."

Clare readily shares with Agnes, Francis's own words regarding the fasting regulations given to the Monastery of San Damiano. The regulations regard fasting and feasts—a difficult concept for Americans who tend to feast daily and fast rarely. Clare's fasting regulations were quite extreme. She fasted at all times on Lenten foods, meaning that she never consumed eggs, milk, milk products, or meat. The sisters of San Damiano ate one full meal a day, except on Sundays and on Christmas when they were permitted to eat twice.

The prescription for Thursdays is an interesting one. Fasting practices were often lightened on Thursdays because it was on this day that the Lord celebrated his Last Supper. In union with the Lord, therefore, one would break one's fast. Clare recommends that each sister make up her own mind according to her health and spirituality concerning the Thursday fast, but her own preference is stated clearly: "Those of us who are healthy fast every day except Sundays and Christmas." She recommends the same for Easter week and for the feasts of Mary and the apostles. The sisters are not obliged to fast on those days except when they fall on a Friday. However, again Clare states, "We who are healthy and strong always eat Lenten fare."

This advice is not about anorexic nuns refusing to eat out of psycho/physical illness. In the monasteries of Assisi and Prague, the monastic table was directly connected with the begging labors of the brothers who lived in quarters connected to these monasteries. Because of the Privilege of Poverty, the sisters shared in the table of the poor. Their fasting was simply the choice to eat as the poor ate and not to use their religious status to take more from the poor than what the poor were truly able to give. Their fasting prohibited the sisters from sharing in a table that belonged to the merchant, noble, or royal classes rather than to the poor.

As Clare will insist, fasting isn't about fasting, it is about poverty. Agnes is to be discreet in her fasting practices. Fasting practices are observed in order to share in the table of the poor—not to break one's health. Sisters who are ill can eat absolutely anything they need in order to help them to feel better.

Clare's farewell is, in a very real sense, an invitation to Agnes to be well. Agnes is to discern her fasting practices so that they will not undermine her health. She is also to discern her spirit and to keep it joyful and glorious before the throne of God.

CONTEMPORARY RELEVANCE

Clare's third letter brings up many issues relevant to our world today. We will organize our reflections around three questions. First, is the connection between choosing poverty as a lifestyle and choosing a daily menu still relevant? Second, how does a Christian discern when to struggle for change and when to wait? Third, what images of eschatological prayer might be helpful for the contemporary Christian?—that is, how can modern Christians place their souls before the glory of God?

Sharing the Table of the Poor

Many Americans are removed from the processes of food production and preparation. We are accustomed to picking something up after work, to driving through for fast food, and to ready-to-bake or even delivered pizza. In many parts of the world, America's relationship, or lack of relationship, with food is seen as strange and even dangerous. In most cultures food and family are still intimately associated, children understand that food comes from the fields and not from the store, and family members spend many hours a day in the preparation of the daily meal.

I was in a small town in Italy not long ago and noticed there a newly built McDonald's near a famous tourist site.

The sign in Italian directing customers through the drive-through made me chuckle. It read: "Enter, Order, Go." In fact, there is no word for fast food in Italian; one has to say the English "fast food." The concept of a drive-through is a foreign concept—as is eating on the run in one's car. Italians must be given instructions, "Enter, Order, Go," so that they can find their way. I rode by this McDonald's many times in my travels but never once saw anyone use the drive-through.

Americans demand food without the work of preparation and often eat in isolation. Food is consumed like gas. We want food on demand, we want food prepared to our liking, and we want food to be affordable. We seldom see the faces behind the food that we eat.

In fact there are many faces. Corporate food companies have undercut scores of family farms. Many American families have had to leave the land after generations of labor. Across the world, small family farmers are struggling to keep their lands out of the grasp of corporate America. When food cannot be harvested by machines, it is often picked by those who are willing to labor cheaply, for long hours in the sun, without protection and often without citizenship. Canning and meat-packing plants are notorious for hiring migrants at cut-rate salaries. One of the most dangerous jobs in America today is working as a meat-packer. Immigrants join students in staffing both fast-food joints and upscale restaurants.

It still costs much more than the customer actually pays to eat beef and pork. Corporate farming requires pestilence protection that runs into rivers, streams, and eventually ground water. Stockyards require stronger and stronger strains of antibiotics that the consumer also ends up eating. It is no secret that American eating habits are threatening to expose us to virulent diseases that, eventually, we may not be able to fight.

How can the contemporary consumer respond? It seems that there are many solutions. Eating simpler food lower on the food chain—what Clare would refer to as fasting foods—surely places us in solidarity with many who labor to feed us with little reward. As an Italian friend of mine often questions: "Why do Americans fill up on meat before they eat their pasta?" Building one's meal around rice, beans, or pasta, as most of the world does, rather than around meat, would create a healthier America.

Surely consciously sharing in the "table of the poor" is a practice that every family could try on a regular basis. Talking with children about the waste of fast food in terms of paper and plastics can help make children more aware of the faces behind their food. Participating in growing and preparing food and in tasting the goodness of homegrown products also builds awareness.

Discerning the Time for Struggle and for Stillness

Everyone seems to have a family member, a boss, a co-worker, or an associate with whom they struggle to be in relationship. Agnes was no exception. She had been trained to be a queen, to run a large household, even to participate in the politics of a rich and prosperous kingdom. After she entered her monastery, important people of power continued to consult her.

Gregory IX, however, found her Franciscan aspirations immature, old-fashioned, and idealistic, and he seemed to have absolutely no qualms about telling her so. At one point, he blatantly tells her to stop her immature behavior and to obey the rule he has given her. While other dignitaries related to Agnes as an equal, Gregory saw her as a subject. In his exasperation, he treats her as a child.

Agnes is justifiably frustrated and angry. She has to politick to get what she wants, and when she does force the papal hand, she gets slapped down with the other. What is perhaps most hurtful is that the religious authority, who once supported her, now looks down on her as a person who is immature and naïve. Agnes, in a sense, has burnt her bridges with Gregory IX. Once the deed is done, there is not much more that she can do.

When Agnes writes to Clare, she is angry with Gregory, and Clare wisely recognizes both that Agnes's anger is justified and that Agnes must move beyond that anger. It is not that Agnes is wrong. In fact, Clare completely agrees with Agnes. The problem is that Agnes is stuck; attachment to anger, even if justified, will not bring holiness. Agnes needs to learn to discern when to act and when to wait. She must also learn how to struggle to obtain the "one thing necessary" and to let go of everything else.

What is the one thing necessary? One needs to follow the path along which God is calling one. There may be struggles in doing that, and those are worth engaging. Beyond this, nothing is worth our peace. There may be struggles, but, if one finds one's home in the glory of God, one can endure these hardships and wait for them to resolve themselves.

Placing One's Soul in the Glory of God

In airports there are often big funnels where children and others can place a penny and watch as it spirals down the funnel and into a tiny hole in the center. If one watches a coin funnel closely, one sees that the coin moves slowly and deliberately at first but gains dizzying momentum and speed as it spirals closer and closer to its demise. Anger is like this. At first, we are uncomfortable with anger. We watch and discern it closely. Soon, however, if unchecked, anger and frustration can spin out of control.

Clare's advice, teaching Agnes how to get out of the spiral of anger and frustration, makes her third letter a masterpiece of spiritual literature. When Agnes writes to Clare she is worried and upset about many things. She is angry with Gregory IX and feels that his stranglehold on the form of life that she, not he, has to live is suffocating her. She feels hopeless and frustrated.

The first thing that Clare does is to stop the penny. She ignores Agnes's issues and talks at length about joy. She answers the factual question on fasting, but refuses to contribute to the energy that is causing Agnes's desolation. When in this desolation, she tells Agnes, "place your mind in the mirror of eternity."

How would a contemporary person do this? Imaging the throne of God surrounded by the angels and the saints with Mary still works for many. Certainly those who pray the Divine Office are used to such images. Other images of God's glory such as light, joy, and peace are certainly possible. What seems necessary is the trinitarian aspect of the image, and for Clare, and for my friend, Margaret, it was important also in one's meditation to place Mary in the scene. For Dom Helder, the singing of the angels was important.

Clare explains what happens to people who take time out of habitual anger in order to place themselves before the heavenly glory. Before they know it, they see the glory of God not only outside of themselves but also as radiating from within themselves. All self-blame, self-degradation, and self-humiliation vanish before the loving eyes of God.

If I had to think of the most healing moment in my life, I would have to claim that it happened to me during confession.

I had gone to confession to a person who knew me well during a very difficult time in my life. I had been belittled and accused, and this had deeply affected my sense of self-worth and self-esteem. Thinking that I was completely to blame, I went to confession hoping for the grace to reform the hopeless corruption of my life.

One by one I revealed what I felt were the character faults that enslaved me. One by one my confessor said, "yes, this is so, but God also sees. . . ." Because the confessor really knew me, very specific examples of what God also saw were given to me. One by one the faults that I was honestly confronting were overshadowed by the glory of God's love that was also shining through me. The confession was healing for me, replacing the mantra, "You're no good, you're no good, you're no good, baby, you're no good," with a simple delight of God's beauty and presence within me.

Clare insists that, if one takes a break from frustrations and imagines oneself before the heavenly glory of God, one will begin to see the glory of God not only externally but also as this glory makes its home within. The fruit of this recognition is, of course, glorious and simple joy. This joy so completely overshadows any external preoccupation that we might have that it becomes the center of our soul rather than anger. Life is no longer defined by our anger but by the glory of God that shines with a new transparency through us.

Questions for Reflection/Sharing

1. How have you practiced seeing the faces behind the food that you eat in your own life? How has this practice changed your eating habits?

2. When have you experienced the need to discern the time for action and for waiting? Is your personality more inclined to action or to waiting? What have been the fruits of action and of waiting in your life?

3. Have you ever tried eschatological prayer? What was difficult for you about this prayer? What images of God's glory have been helpful to your prayer?

Clare's Fourth Letter to Agnes

INTRODUCTION

The conflict between the papacy and Frederick II erupted, and travel between Italy and Bohemia became gravely dangerous. It was fifteen years before Clare would write to Agnes again. When Clare does write, she is on her deathbed with her blood-sister, Agnes of Assisi, at her side.

Clare has seen the Franciscan movement grow from a few brothers with oral permission to preach to an order of thousands of brothers, sisters, and laypeople eager to follow the canonized and very famous merchant from Assisi. The friars have been promoted to serve as papal ambassadors, royal chaplains, nuncios, inquisitors, missionaries, university professors, and more. They had built immense churches and large friaries. Needing to gain credibility among those with power for their expanding ministries and offices, the friars progressively mitigated their dedication to poverty. Both Gregory IX and Innocent IV were happy to accommodate the needed changes and provided the friars with the means necessary to solicit and manage large sums of money and properties.

While many monasteries within Gregory IX's Order of Poor Ladies were happy to receive landed endowments and other treasures securing their monasteries, Clare and Agnes held fast to their Privilege of Poverty. Political upheavals had brought hardships to both monasteries, and Agnes of Prague's monastery would suffer even more deeply the hardship of poverty after Clare's death.

During the intervening years, Innocent IV had occasionally written to Agnes in order to solicit the aid of the king of Bohemia. Agnes, of course, readily cooperated, but not without asking from the Pope favors in return. In this way, little by little, Agnes carved out the way for a specifically Franciscan identity for her monastery. Not only had she secured the Privilege of Poverty but she had also received fasting regulations for her monastery consistent with those at the Monastery of San Damiano and had widened the permissions of the friars to enter, preach, and serve the sisters of her monastery.

In her fourth letter, Clare writes to the sister who is "the other half of her soul." Its eschatological tone is reminiscent of one preparing for death. Clare is confident of heaven because she has kept her pact with the Poor Christ and with his promise: "Blessed are the poor in spirit, for theirs is the kingdom of heaven" (Matt 5:3).

CLARE'S FOURTH LETTER

(1) To the other half of her soul and repository of the special love of her deepest heart, illustrious queen, spouse of the Lamb of the eternal King, the Lady Agnes, her own dearest mother and, among all the others, her special daughter, (2) Clare, unworthy servant of Christ and

useless handmaid of his handmaids who live in the Monastery of San Damiano in Assisi, (3) sends greetings and her prayer that Agnes, together with the other most holy virgins, will sing a new song before the throne of God and of the Lamb, and will follow the Lamb wherever he goes.

(4) O mother and daughter, spouse of the King of all ages, even if I have not written to you as frequently as both your soul and mine would have desired and longed for, do not for a moment wonder (5) or believe in any way that the fire of my love for you burns any less sweetly in the deepest heart of your mother. (6) The truth is that a shortage of messengers and the obvious perils of travel have hindered me. (7) But now, as I write to your love, I rejoice and exult for you in the joy of the Spirit, spouse of Christ, (8) because like that other most holy virgin, Saint Agnes, you have been in an astonishing way espoused to the Immaculate Lamb, who, having assumed responsibility for all the vanities of this world, takes away the sins of the world.

(9) Happy, indeed, is the one permitted to share
in this Sacred Banquet so as to be joined
with all the feelings of her heart to him

(10) whose beauty all the blessed hosts of the
heavens unceasingly admire,

(11) whose affection moves,
whose contemplation invigorates,
whose generosity fills,

(12) whose sweetness replenishes,
whose remembrance pleasantly brings light,

(13) whose fragrance will revive the dead,
and whose glorious vision will bless
all the citizens of the heavenly Jerusalem,

(14) because the vision of him is the splendor of
everlasting glory,
the radiance of everlasting light,
and a mirror without tarnish.

(15) Look into this mirror every day, O queen,
spouse of Jesus Christ, and continually examine your
face in it, (16) so that in this way you may adorn yourself completely, inwardly and outwardly, clothed and
covered in multicolored apparel, (17) adorned in the
same manner with flowers and garments made of all the
virtues as is proper, dearest daughter and spouse of the
Most High King. (18) Moreover, in this mirror shine
blessed poverty, holy humility, and charity beyond
words, as you will be able, with God's grace, to contemplate throughout the entire mirror.

(19) Look closely, I say, to the beginning of the
life of this admired one, indeed at the poverty of him
who was wrapped in swaddling clothes and placed in a
manger. (20) O marvelous humility! O astonishing
poverty! (21) The King of the angels, the Lord of
heaven and earth is laid to rest in a manger! (22) Consider also the midst of his life, his humility, or at least
his blessed poverty, the countless hardships, and the
punishments that he endured for the redemption of
the human race. (23) Indeed, ponder the final days of
this mirrored one, contemplate the ineffable love with
which he was willing to suffer on the tree of the cross
and to die there a kind of death that is more shameful
than any other.

(24) That mirror suspended upon the wood of the
cross kept urging from there those passing by to consider this, saying: (25) O all you who pass by this way,

look and see if there is any suffering like my suffering. (26) In response let us with one voice and in one spirit answer him who is crying out and lamenting: I will remember this over and over and my soul will sink within me. (27) Therefore, seeing this, O queen of the Heavenly King, you must burn ever more strongly with the fervor of charity!

(28) Furthermore, as you contemplate his indescribable delights, riches, and everlasting honors, (29) and heaving a sigh because of your heart's immeasurable desire and love may you exclaim:

(30) Draw me after you, Heavenly Spouse, we shall run in the fragrance of your perfumes!

(31) I shall run and not grow weary until you bring me into the wine cellar,

(32) until your left hand is under my head, and your right arm blissfully embraces me; and you kiss me with the most blissful kiss of your mouth.

(33) As you are placed in this contemplation, may you remember your poor, little mother, (34) knowing that I have inseparably inscribed the happy memory of you on the tablets of my heart, for I regard you as dearer than all others.

(35) What more can be said? Let my physical tongue be silent, as it is said, and let the tongue of the Spirit speak. (36) O blessed daughter, since in no way at all could my bodily tongue express more fully the love that I have for you, (37) that which I have written is certainly inadequate. I beg you to receive these words with kindness and devotion, seeing in them at least the motherly affection, by which every day I am stirred by the fire of

love for you and your daughters; please ask them to pray for me and my daughters in Christ. (38) Indeed, inasmuch as they are able, my own daughters, and especially the most prudent virgin, Agnes, our sister, beg you and your daughters to pray for them in the Lord.

(39) Farewell, dearest daughter, together with your own daughters, until we meet at the throne of glory of the great God, and pray for us.

(40) I must now commend to your charity, as fully as possible, our dearest bearers of this letter, Brother Amato, beloved by God and human beings, and Brother Bonaugura. Amen.

CONTEXT

Frederick II continued to press his bid to obtain central Italy by force. Gregory IX died on August 22, 1241, with the emperor's army surrounding Rome. The papacy was in shambles.

After Innocent IV became pope on June 28, 1243, Agnes immediately wrote to congratulate him, and to ask him to consider her as a spiritual daughter. The Pope wrote back saying that he was pleased to do so. Seeing this cordial beginning as a possible opening to again press for a specifically Franciscan Rule and constitutions, Agnes immediately wrote back to the Pope asking "that the two phrases which are written regarding 'the virtue of obedience' and 'the Rule of Benedict' be removed from that form and that we have those indulgences that were specially granted to the aforesaid monastery by Pope Gregory recorded in it."

There is much more at stake here than a simple legalism. Agnes is worried that Innocent IV might disregard previous privileges and that her form of life will again be compromised. It would be so much easier if she could simply have the privileges given to her monastery placed within the monastic constitutions.

The Policies of Innocent IV

Unfortunately, Innocent IV was aware of, and seems to have agreed completely with, the policies of Gregory IX in regard to women's monasteries. In a letter of November 13, 1243, he flatly denied Agnes's request. He also mitigated the fasting laws for the monastery of Prague even further than Gregory IX had done. He repeats the same objections to Agnes's request given by Gregory and then attempts to explain to Agnes that the phrases that concern her are merely juridical necessities that have no real impact on the lives of her sisters. Professing the Rule of St. Benedict has no real meaning for the sisters, according to Innocent, other than obedience, the relinquishment of personal property, and chastity. Even today one can feel the lump in Agnes's throat when one reads his letter.

> The addition about the Rule of Saint Benedict has been made so that your form of religious life would be found authentic, as though contained in that Rule which is, as it were, distinguished among approved forms of religious life. No necessity has been introduced because of these words that would hold you to observe that Rule. This is clearly proven by the fact that our above-mentioned predecessor declared in the presence and hearing of our venerable brother, the Bishop of Ostia, that this Rule does not bind the sisters of your Order

to anything other than obedience, the giving up of personal property, and perpetual chastity.

Agnes had waited many years for a change in the papal policy. Innocent IV had no interest in change. He understood that there were some women like Clare and Agnes who still wanted to follow the "old" way of living the Franciscan life. Innocent's papacy was challenged by difficulties on every side. He was warring against Germans, Muslims, Tartars, and heretics. He was sending Franciscan brothers to every part of the known world as diplomats and nuncios. He was interested in the internal difficulties of the Franciscan Order only if these difficulties impeded the papal mission. He had answered Agnes's question, and he didn't want to be bothered with these trivial matters again.

> Thus may you, peaceful dove and virtuous daughter, be at ease and put a stop to the disturbances of your mind. Do not take up the notion of asking similar questions about other matters, since it suffices for you and these same sisters for meriting the rewards of everlasting life that with pure hearts for the glory of God you observe only this often-mentioned formula with the assistance of apostolic dispensations.

Apparently Agnes's monastery was not the only monastery of Poor Sisters who had difficulty professing their lives according to a rule that was, in the eyes of the Pope, a mere legalism. About nine months later, Innocent wrote a letter to the entire Order of Saint Damian concerning the objection that some of the sisters had to the phrase, "the Rule of St. Benedict." Innocent IV repeated his minimalist interpretation of these words and told the sisters "to put an end to the disturbance of your minds."

Perhaps to confirm the policy once and for all, Innocent IV issued his own version of Gregory IX's constitutions on

November 13, 1245. This apparently produced a great consternation among the sisters because on August 6, 1247, Innocent did an about-face. He changed the Rule of St. Benedict to the Rule of St. Francis and placed the sisters under the authority of the minister general of the Order of Friars Minor or, if the minister chose, under the provincial of their respective provinces.

Facing the Question of Poverty

It seems that Clare and Agnes finally had their hard-won desire. Unfortunately, the case was not quite so simple. By November of 1245, the Franciscan brothers had mitigated their poverty to such an extent that it was easier for the papacy to support the sisters following the Franciscan Rule than to give them the much more radical Privilege of Poverty. Because of the mitigations in the Franciscan Rule itself, Innocent IV sees no discrepancy between giving the sisters the Rule of St. Francis and legislating for common property and revenues. He gives the sisters the same sort of Franciscan poverty that the brothers were then following: "In addition, you may have permission to receive, hold, and freely retain revenue and possessions in common. When appropriate, each monastery of your Order is to have one prudent and trustworthy procurator who shall deal with these possessions in the manner described."

From a juridical point of view, the tweaking of Gregory IX's constitutions to fit the charismatic inspirations of individual monasteries by means of dispensations had created anything but the hoped for uniformity. The papacy wanted easy legal maintenance for nuns. It was preoccupied with complex issues that would determine its very survival. It wanted monasteries of nuns to be self-sufficient financially.

It no longer wanted to deal with endless privileges and exemptions that brought further complexity. Innocent IV summarized his position quite well: "An even more important reason was that many diverse types of dispensations have already been made regarding that Rule, the result being that there seems to be not one, but many professions."

There were also monasteries of sisters who did not wish to accept the Rule of St. Francis. Fearing the pauperistic aspirations of Clare and Agnes, some sisters in the Order of Saint Damian asked to retain the Rule of St. Benedict. What had been so precisely orchestrated by so many expert jurists had erupted into a terrible mess.

Finally in a letter written on June 6, 1250, to the cardinal of Ostia, Innocent IV admits that the Order of St. Damian is not a united order and is, in fact, following two rules. In regard to those sisters who wish to retain the Rule of St. Benedict, the cardinal is to "see to it that the old formula that they accepted at the creation of their Order be observed by them inviolably if an advantage to their souls may be better gained by it."

The Rule of Clare

Innocent IV personally visited Clare at the Monastery of San Damiano sometime between August 1–8, 1253. Clare was on her deathbed. While the form of life written by Innocent was based on the Franciscan Rule, it did not outline the "living without possessions" as central to Clare's vocation. Since the Order of St. Damian was now effectively two orders, one following the Rule of St. Benedict and the other following the Rule of St. Francis, the monasteries connected in spirit with San Damiano could now be formulated in their own particular charismatic and juridical base.

In her Rule, Clare places the issue that has been so crucial to the story of her life—poverty—at the very center. If a woman wishes to enter the Monastery of San Damiano, she must "sell all that she has and take care to distribute the proceeds to the poor." Having seen how both papacy and the brothers have mitigated and interpreted Francis's ideal of poverty after his death, Clare is careful to spell out exactly what she has in mind in regard to the particular sort of poverty to be lived in her monastery.

> The abbesses who shall succeed me in office and all the sisters are bound to observe poverty inviolably to the end: that is to say, by not receiving or having possession or ownership either for themselves or through an intermediary, or having anything that might reasonably be called property, except as much land as necessity requires for the integrity and proper seclusion of the monastery, and this land may not be cultivated except as a garden for the needs of the sisters.

Clare's practice of personal and corporate poverty is clear. Before entering, the sisters are to sell everything and give the proceeds to the poor rather than to bring their dowries as patrimony to the monastery. They are not to engage in the practice of having procurators. The monastery is to be surrounded only by enough land necessary for its seclusion. Only the land necessary to provide for the vegetative needs of the sisters of the monastery may be cultivated. In other words, the land of the monastery is under no circumstances to be used to provide regular income for the monastery.

Clare's Fourth Letter to Agnes

There is no mention of Clare's Rule in the fourth letter or of the papal visit, so perhaps Clare's letter is written before August 1, 1253. Clare's tenderness and love for the sister that she has known only from afar is evident from the beginning until the end of this letter.

Clare begins by calling Agnes "the other half of her soul," "the repository of the special love of her deepest heart," "her own dearest mother," and "among all the others, her special daughter." The eschatological theme of the letter is presented in the salutation. Agnes is to sing a new song before the throne of God.

Quoting the *Legend of St. Agnes of Rome,* Clare sings of the glory found before the throne of God. The advice that Clare had given Agnes in the third letter regarding placing herself before the throne of God in prayer, Clare had apparently practiced herself. Clare will continue in this letter to give Agnes even more instructions concerning the life of Franciscan prayer.

Christ As a Mirror

Agnes is to look into the mirror who is Christ every day, and she is to continually examine her own face in this mirror. By looking at Christ, Agnes will be able to adorn herself both inwardly and outwardly in a variety of virtues. Most precious of all is the poverty, humility, and charity of Christ that shine through the mirror and reflect upon the face of the one peering into it.

Clare next gives Agnes instructions on how she is to follow in the footsteps of Christ in prayer. Perhaps the clearest and most precious account of Franciscan prayer in the entire early Franciscan corpus, Clare's fourth letter asks Agnes to follow Christ in the four stages of his life.

One begins by placing oneself before the manger. Franciscan prayer begins by contemplating Christmas! Clare advises

Agnes to contemplate especially the poverty of the baby lying in the manger. At the thought of the infant Christ, Clare immediately breaks into song: "O marvelous humility! O astonishing poverty! The King of the angels, the Lord of heaven and earth is laid to rest in a manger!"

Second, Agnes is to meditate on the adult life of Christ. Most especially, she is to consider his humility, poverty, and the countless hardships he endured for our redemption. Third, she is to ponder Christ's final days, considering the love with which he was willing to suffer on the cross, and the shamefulness of his death. Fourth, Agnes is to contemplate Christ in glory.

Accepting the Contempt of Poverty

The third comment of Clare needs to be considered seriously. The choice of poverty places those who are perhaps used to being in the middle and upper classes on the same level as the poor. While those with resources might initially admire the choice of poverty, poverty that is lived out day by day invites contempt. The clothes, table, and lifestyle of the person who chooses poverty do not fit in well with the expectations of the rich. In her second letter Clare wrote:

> Now that you have made yourself contemptible in this world for his sake, look upon and the follow the one who made himself contemptible for your sake. Gaze upon, examine, contemplate, most noble queen, desiring to follow your Spouse, who is more beautiful than the sons of humankind, and who for your salvation became the vilest of men, despised, struck, and flogged repeatedly over his entire body, dying while suffering the excruciating torments of the cross.

We remember that Agnes had been surprised when she discovered that Gregory IX seemed not to respect her as a royal woman after she had insisted on being faithful to her choice of poverty. Like many who choose to embrace poverty, Agnes thought of her decision as a noble one. Every day in her own backyard, the poor of Prague were being fed because of Agnes's choice.

To Gregory IX, however, Agnes was becoming a nuisance. He was grateful that the Franciscans were able to capture the hearts of the common people and thus keep them out of the hands of the heretics. Gregory was willing to mitigate the demands of poverty so that the friars could teach, preach, and minister more effectively. As for the women, Gregory wanted well-organized and self-sufficient monasteries. He wanted the sisters to have reputations for holiness. He wanted them to live a disciplined and edifying lifestyle. Poverty can undermine religious discipline, and Gregory had seen firsthand the consequences of poverty among nuns. He preferred a balanced lifestyle rather than a risky one.

Those who choose poverty, need to remember that they are choosing contempt. How does one endure this contempt without becoming bitter? Clare's suggestion is a simple one. In prayer, contemplate the contempt that Christ endured for the redemption of humanity. As one places oneself in the scene pondering the crucifixion, one will hear Christ cry out: "O all you who pass by this way, look and see if there is any suffering like my suffering."

The Privilege of Poverty

Medievals loved the biblical Song of Songs, allegorized it, and frequently quoted it. At first glance it seems as though Clare simply follows this pattern of quoting the Song of Songs to describe the intimacy of Christ with a religious.

Medieval literature pictured the soul of the faithful person being brought into the wine cellar in order to celebrate intimacy with God. But Clare is not simply mimicking other medieval writers. Her spirituality is unique, and it is always, in the end, about her choice of poverty. The key to her meaning is in the embrace itself. Clare writes: "I shall run and not grow weary until you bring me into the wine cellar, until your left hand is under my head and your right arm blissfully embraces me; and you kiss me with the most blissful kiss of your mouth."

In the Privilege of Poverty that Clare had obtained from Gregory IX, the "left hand" of the Spouse supports the Poor Ladies in their choice of poverty. In particular it upholds the weaknesses of the body that need to be supported in the choice of poverty: "The lack of goods from this proposal does not frighten you, for the left hand of your Heavenly Spouse is under your head to uphold the weaknesses of your body that you have submitted to the law of the soul through your well-ordered love."

It is usually the fear of lacking bodily essentials that makes most people stop before giving all their riches to the poor as the Gospel suggests. How will one eat? Where will one stay? How will one pay for health care and retirement costs? These are real considerations, and these questions must be discerned carefully according to each person's vocation. For the Franciscan, Clare suggests that peace is found in the experience of Christ's left arm supporting one concretely in the experience of poverty. It is God himself who will give the beloved bread, health, and even love.

Clare and Agnes are able to embrace poverty because they are convinced at the core of their being that God is a good business partner. What one gives to God will be given back a hundredfold. The intimacy of Christ's left arm embracing his beloved sister assures Clare and Agnes that God will not abandon them. Like any marriage, union with Christ demands that one trust one's very economic well-being to another. To fail to do this is to fail to enter into complete intimacy with God.

In the Privilege of Poverty, the "right arm" of the beloved from the Song of Songs is the eschatological reward given to those who persevere in poverty. Not only will Christ provide his beloved with daily bread needed for physical life and nourishment, but he will offer himself as food to his beloved. In eternity, intimacy with God will be the only food needed for the beloved whose love and desire for God will be completely satisfied.

> Accordingly, he who feeds the birds of the sky and clothes the lilies of the field will not fail you in matters of food and of clothing until, passing among you, he serves himself to you in eternity, when indeed his right arm will more blissfully embrace you in the greatness of his vision.

In his commentary on the Song of Songs, Gregory the Great had used the left arm of the beloved to symbolize the present life and the right arm to symbolize eternal life. What is odd in Clare's text is the word "blissfully." Both Song of Songs 2:6 and 8:3 read: "His left hand is under my head, and his right arm embraces me." There is no "blissfully" in the original text. The word "blissfully" is found only in the Privilege of Poverty, which undoubtedly was Clare's reference.

As we have seen throughout Clare's letters, Clare's spirituality is a simple one. Her nuns are not pondering the depths of the mysticism of Bernard of Clairvaux or of Hugh of St. Victor. Their spiritual instruction comes from sermons, and their spiritual program is very much determined by their poverty. Work, as well as prayer, is essential to their survival. This prayer, however, is a prayer of simply following in the footsteps of Jesus. One gazes, considers, and contemplates the four moments of Christ's life: his birth, his life, his death, and his eternal glory.

In pondering Christ's eternal glory, Clare sees that Christ is her eternal food. We remember that Clare places herself in prayer in the glory of eternity, and therefore has enjoyed knowing Christ intimately as food for her soul. Through such prayer the boundaries between this life and the next become blurred. One is happy, as Paul insists, in life and in death. Clare credits her precious Privilege of Poverty as the key to this intimacy with Christ.

Clare's Mysticism

Some authors have questioned whether or not Clare was a mystic. How could a woman with few documented visions, no raptures, and few other extraordinary gifts be considered a mystic? In a sense Clare's spirituality is too simple, too plain.

Clare's spiritual depth is proven most radically by her utter commitment to poverty. For those who choose physical poverty and then faithfully live and grow in love with the Poor Christ, God does not need to cut through as many layers of delusion. They are what they are before God, nothing more and nothing less. Perhaps an example will make this clear.

I was on my way to a party when I received a call from one of our sisters who lives in a home for street women. One of the women in the house had died. Her recovery had been moving along very well, but a reoccurring infection cropped up, and the doctors, even to their surprise, lost her in the struggle. Our sister had opened the house just before Sept. 11, 2001, and the already minimal budget for the house was stretched to the maximum.

Thankfully, the Episcopalians in the area agreed to have a service and pay for the burial expenses for the woman, but there were still other needs. The women living in the Catholic Worker House had seen one of their dear sisters lose the struggle. They needed to be encouraged to choose life, and this encouragement would need to take the form of relieving the very real poverty of the house for awhile.

I went to the party very preoccupied about all of this and was reaching for a soda when a woman cornered me and started speaking to me of the dark night of the soul that she was experiencing. It was a very dark one, and my throat was really dry. One half hour later, I still really needed the soda, but she still had me in a corner, and the darkness showed no sign of abating soon. Finally a friend came to greet me, and I was able to wriggle my way out of the corner.

The woman was writing beautiful poetry about the depths and intimacy of her dark night. She was, as my students would say, "all about it!" On the other hand, my sister who was scrambling and begging throughout the neighborhood in order to help our women survive was praying simply and desperately for daily bread. Hers was a simple prayer. When she went to bed at night, the Lord did not need to cut through her illusions by means of mystic darkness. The stench of urine in the hallways, and the contempt of other people, even some religious people, toward her because of the company that she had chosen to keep had accomplished that years ago. When she went to bed, she daily handed the whole impossible mess over to God. While the woman in the dark night twisted and turned, the sister with the cracked walls slept soundly.

The wonder of God is that all are invited to union and that we are invited along paths that best suit us. For those who are invited along paths that keep them within the mainstream of society, God must often use the knife of darkness to cut through illusions. For those who have embraced poverty with freedom and maturity, God's work is in a sense simpler and in a way more delightful. God merely needs to provide daily bread and to become the daily bread that feeds.

Clare spent her life caring and providing for her sisters. She comforted them when they were sick, multiplied bread when they were hungry, covered them at night from the cold in the dormitory, and listened to their hearts. She delighted in the simple patch of flowers that provided color to their humble chapel. Her prayer placed her before her beloved Christ in his birth, life, death, and glory.

At the end of her *Interior Castle,* after she has described the prayer of quiet, the prayer of rapture, locutions, flights of the spirit, etc., Teresa of Avila describes the depths of mystical union with a simple formula. Mystical union for Teresa is simply that God takes care of the person's business, and the person takes care of God's business. In other words, mystical union for Teresa is simply the *sacrum commercium*—the holy business deal.

How God prepares us for divine union does not matter. What matters is that in the end all true mysticism is profoundly simple. It is a love affair that demands looking at the other, both in the needs of our neighbor and in prayer, and being concerned simply with the other. One person might be led to give up everything to serve the poorest of the poor. Another person finds herself totally dedicated to raising children, fulfilling the needs of a husband, and juggling a job besides. Another may be led in prayer to utter darkness, so that she might fall in love not with the consolations of God, but with the God of consolation. In the end, if one is faithful to one's vocational calling, one can learn to love by taking any one of these paths. Mysticism is simply the ability to love another totally, simply, freely, and joyfully.

The Mysticism of Affection

Clare expresses her ability to love the other totally as she says her farewell to the sister who has been so faithful to the Franciscan vision. Agnes is asked to remember Clare in prayer, but Clare does not discuss her dying pains. She is preoccupied with the care and concern that she has for Agnes. She knows how difficult it will be for Agnes not to have Clare to turn to, even if their relationship had been only through letters. Clare has the memory of Agnes "inseparably inscribed" on the tablets of her heart. Clare assures Agnes that she loves her and the sisters in Prague as a mother.

Another sister will miss Clare terribly, although, in fact, she will die shortly after Clare. Clare's blood-sister, Agnes of Assisi, is at Clare's side. The Monastery of San Damiano is losing the sister who has been its heart and soul. Clare does not regret leaving them but rather entrusts the sisters in Prague and the sisters in Assisi to the care of each other. The sisters in Prague must love, pray for, and cherish the sisters in Assisi and vice versa. One can hear in Clare's words, the words of Jesus: "Love one another, as I have loved you" (John 15:12).

Even on her deathbed, Clare is filled with simple humor. She asks Agnes to take good care of the brothers who are delivering her letter to Prague. Their names are most likely nicknames. Brother Amato means "beloved by God," and Brother Bonaugura means "good wishes," and "farewell." Agnes's very grief will be transformed by caring for and receiving with every kindness the brothers whom Clare is sending to her.

Agnes's Continued Fidelity

After Clare's death, a new pope, Gregory X, again wanted Agnes to accept endowments for her monastery. The Second Council of Lyons, May 7–July 7, 1274, addressed its twenty-third constitution to religious orders, placing Agnes's monastery in jeopardy. The Church was not comfortable with monastic foundations that were not well endowed, and it wanted to put an end to them once and for all. The council decreed:

> As to those Orders, however, confirmed by the Apostolic See and instituted after the council, whose profession, rule, or constitutions forbid them to have revenues or possessions for their fitting support but whose insecure mendicancy usually provides a living through public begging, we decree that they may survive on the following terms. The professed members of these Orders may continue in them if they are willing not to admit henceforth anyone to profession, nor to acquire a new house or land, nor to have power to alienate the houses or land they have, without special leave of the Apostolic See.

Most likely working to execute the decrees of the council, Cardinal Legate John Cajetan wrote to Agnes asking her to accept possessions on account of the "evils of the age and the threatening dangerous times." *The Legend of Agnes of Prague* records Agnes's response: "She resisted with a courageous spirit, much preferring to be without anything, voluntarily accepting all want and destitution rather than to depart in any way from the poverty of Christ who became poor for our sake."

It does not seem that Agnes ever submitted to John Cajetan's request. Since the Order of Friars Minor had been exempted from the above constitution, perhaps Agnes also claimed, since she now lived under the Rule of St. Francis, that her monastery was also exempt. As late as the 1390s, Bartholomew Rinonico of Pisa states: "Up until today in the city of Prague where Agnes was a sister, those sisters, although from nobility and numerous, have no property and no income, but live on alms that are begged for them by the brothers."

In any case, by 1274, the question of accumulating possessions for the Prague monastery was becoming moot. Agnes's nephew Otakar II was now the Bohemian king. Hoping to gain advantage from the increasing wealth and prominence of Bohemia, he aspired to be chosen as the next German emperor. Instead, Gregory X snubbed him, and chose an unknown, Duke Rudolph of Habsburg.

From the beginning of his reign, Rudolph undermined the wealth and influence of Otakar II. In response, the Bohemian king prepared for war and in the process lost the support of many of the Bohemian nobles and foreign allies. When he died in battle in 1278, Bohemia was left without leadership. Rudolph took full advantage of the situation. Flood and famine in 1279–80 further devastated the Bohemian countryside. Many of the poor in Prague died of hunger and disease.

It is said that when Agnes died, almost twenty years after Clare on March 2, 1282, the sisters laid her body out for two weeks behind the grating of the sister's chapel. The poor of the city thronged to the monastery longing to see her and to find comfort in her presence for one last time. It was precisely because Agnes insisted on her vocational right to live "without possessions," that she found herself to be, during the last years of her life, the only member of the royal family permitted to live in Bohemia. During her lifetime, she saw her hospital foundation grow and expand, providing the poor with an excellent system of social care that still exists today. Although Clare and Agnes were required to live under the Rule of St. Benedict for much of their lives, there was no question in their minds or in ours that they were, in fact, Franciscans.

CONTEMPORARY RELEVANCE

Clare began her Franciscan life with a very simple vision. She had seen firsthand the violence of greed and wealth, and she wanted to live a peaceful life. Instead of entering into the culture of wealth with its accompanying violence, she chose a life of poverty. In doing so she gave away her resources to the poor and in her own small way turned society upside down, if only for a moment.

Agnes also, with all her worldly wealth and potential prestige as a Bohemian royal, gave everything away so that the resources of the rich might truly belong to the poor. What she didn't expect was that other religious people would spurn her and disregard her largely because of her choice. Her choice made Gregory IX nervous. He would have been happier if her choice had been less radical, perhaps, even in a backhanded way, less judgmental of his own life.

Obviously most people do not have the freedom that Clare and Agnes had in being able to give all their possessions away to the poor and to join the poor in their lifestyle. Can those with families and responsibilities still appreciate and, in a small sense, follow the spiritual insights of these first Franciscan women?

I once worked in an immersion program in Milwaukee, run by the Capuchins. This program is designed to help people who do not live in the central city make connections with those who do. The program offers immersion experiences in jail ministry, mental health ministry, food pantry and clothing ministry, and soup-kitchen ministry.

We would introduce people to different ministries and then would have them meet and talk with people who were involved in these ministries. We would go to the jail and listen to stories, hear the life journeys of those suffering from the purgatory of schizophrenia, and sit down and eat with those enjoying a meal at the soup kitchen. Such experiences, of course, opened the eyes of those who participated—but the experience wasn't designed merely to open eyes.

During the last two sessions of the experience, those participating were invited to enter into a discernment process to find where they felt God was calling them in relationship to the ministries that they had seen. Some people knew immediately where they were called. Others floundered. Anything they envisioned themselves doing seemed very small. What difference would it make?

There was an older Capuchin, who had worked in the central city nearly all of his life, who would take those who were floundering aside and tell them simply, "Just do one thing. It won't be the greatest thing; it won't be the most important thing, but just do one thing."

In a sense, Clare and Agnes's life was about "just doing one thing." They had decided that they were called to give what they had to the poor and not to take it back. Their lives were about living the consequences of that choice. These consequences included being misjudged and even spurned by others including popes, some of Francis's own brothers, and in Clare's case, her own family. They learned how to suffer contempt in union with Christ who also suffered contempt because he chose to enter into our poverty.

Those who choose poverty are to receive a hundredfold even in this life. Clare and Agnes's choice of poverty helped them reach the heights of mystical union where love of God and neighbor occupy one's entire energy and vision and give one delight. Both were blessed to live with sisters who shared their life and their vision. Both shared in the delights of having the Franciscan brothers sing with them the Divine Office, celebrate the liturgy with them, and offer them their words of preaching. Both were able to bring comfort and healing to those who came to their monasteries for assistance. Both were loved and cherished by the poor.

Clare and Agnes just did one thing, the one thing that God called them to do, and they lived this vocation in fidelity. Their perseverance gained for them union with God and a true love of their neighbor. Although their lives were filled with hardships and difficulties, Agnes and Clare were known in life and in death for their joy and peace. This is so because they practiced taking refuge from self-depreciating judgments and learned to "listen to the angels sing." Through spending time following Christ in his birth, life, death, and glory in prayer, they learned to feel at home in God's presence and to see the wonder of God's glory emanating from their own souls. Celebrating the wonder of their creation, they gathered the poor together. The worth of their lives was not measured in terms of honor, power, and riches, but in the glory of God freely given to all who ask. They were simply who they were before God, nothing more and nothing less.

Questions for Reflection/Sharing

1. Have you ever experienced God providing for your physical needs? How can Christians discern when to

prudently plan for their needs and when to trust God to provide for their needs?

2. Have you experienced the *sacrum commercium*—God takes care of your business, while you take care of God's business—in your own life?

3. How have Clare's letters spoken to your heart? Has your life and prayer changed since you met Clare?

Choosing Poverty

A Contemporary Choice

We have seen that Clare's mysticism is a practical mysticism: "Go, sell your possessions, and give the money to the poor, and you will have treasure in heaven; then come, follow me" (Matt 19:21). After Clare hears Francis preach these words of Scripture to her, she sells what she has and gives it to the poor. Clare prayerfully follows Christ by putting herself before him as a baby lying in the manger, by following him lovingly during his public life, by staying beside him as he dies on the cross, and by adoring the depths of his heavenly glory.

Most of us like Clare's mysticism. We admire the depth of Clare's prayer. It's the first step in Clare's spirituality that makes us hesitate, stumble, find excuses—"sell what you have and give it to the poor."

Certainly not every Christian is called, as Clare was, to follow this Scripture passage literally. For instance, those with responsibilities of children cannot ordinarily sell everything that they have and give it to the poor. Francis knew this, and when people with families asked him how they might best follow the Gospel, Francis told them to live

moral and honest lives, to love their neighbors, and to practice their faith. God does not give everyone the same call.
God calls each one by name, each one specially for God's
greater glory. Fidelity requires that we discern God's call and
follow the path of our own call with our whole hearts.

Even today, however, there are still those who hear the
Lord speaking clearly to them saying: "Go, sell everything,
and give it to the poor." This call, like every other one, must
be followed wholeheartedly. We see the fruits of this call in
the lives of Francis, Clare, Elizabeth of Hungary, Agnes of
Prague, Anthony of Padua, Agnes of Assisi, Dorothy Day,
and so many others. Like all vocational calls, the call to
poverty needs to be appreciated and supported by the Christian community.

At first glance, the call to poverty seems contradictory.
Why should people of means give everything away only to
beg from others? Isn't this behavior irresponsible, even absurd? Aren't there enough poor people in this world? Why
would anyone deliberately wish to increase the ranks of the
poor by irrevocably fleeing from wealth? Wouldn't it be better for those who want to do good deeds to invest their
wealth wisely and enjoy the fruits of their investments with
the poor?

Justification for the gospel invitation becomes clearer
when we look at the lives of those who have wholeheartedly
lived the call to poverty. Agnes of Prague, for example, gave
away her royal dowry and joined the ranks of Prague's poor.
As a result, the poor and the sick of Prague were cared for
and fed at the hospital that Agnes built. This work continues even today. Agnes made her home with the poor and
shared in their plight, enabling her brother, King Wenceslaus I,
to have direct information concerning the needs of the poor.

Agnes, because she was actually walking the walk, no doubt begged for even more resources for the poor during her lifetime from the royal and noble families of Prague. When the royal family was exiled from Prague, Agnes, who was of no threat to the new regime, but who was a symbol of Bohemian sovereignty, was able to stay with her beloved people. Even today there is a belief in Prague that when the body of Agnes is found again (it was lost somehow between the medieval floods and the Hussite rebellions) life will be better for Prague's poor.

Clare and Agnes became poor because Christ became poor for us. They were not trying to live out some sort of philosophy. Although Clare and Agnes would have agreed with the axiom, "live simply, so that others can simply live," the motivation for their lives was much more profound. Clare personally understood that one found trinitarian joy by entering into the depths of Christ's poverty. We find this joy at the core of our being, but we see it only when we come face to face with our poverty and when we experience the contempt that good people have toward us precisely because of our poverty. In coming before God in our poverty, we see the glory of God not only outside of ourselves, but also radiating from within ourselves.

Each of us, within the contexts of our own vocations, must hear and respond to the call of the poor. By listening to the voice of the Poor Christ in the very practical needs of our neighbors, we identify with, rather than persecute, the Poor Christ and in this way enter into his glory. By "doing just one thing," we begin to even out the divide between the rich and the poor. By emptying ourselves of our worries, our insecurities, and yes, of our resources, we find treasures that fill our emptiness in a way that material riches cannot.

In the end, the choice of poverty is simply the choice of being who we are before God, nothing more and nothing less. We come into this world naked, and we leave this world without our stocks, bonds, and other riches that will do us no good on the other side. We need to exchange our earthly riches for a currency that has value both on earth and in heaven—the love of God and the love of neighbor. We need to focus our energies on doing God's business and to rejoice at the wondrous outpouring of God's abundant love and grace in our daily lives.

Questions for Reflection/Sharing

1. After reading Clare's letters, how will your response to the needs of the poor change? How does this response fit into your primary vocational commitment?

2. Clare's spirituality can perhaps be best summed up in the Scripture passage: "Go, sell everything that you have, and give it to the poor. Then, come follow me." If you had to choose a Scripture passage that best summed up your own spirituality, what would it be and why?

3. Since we cannot take the riches of this world with us when we die, how, practically, are you planning to exchange your own resources for those that will have value on the other side? Have your practical decisions regarding this world's resources changed since you have met Clare?